APRIL

Make the Most of Every Month with Carson-Dellosa's Monthly Books!

Production Manager
Chris McIntyre

Editorial Director
Jennifer Weaver-Spencer

Writers
Lynette Pyne
Amy Gamble
Trisha Yates

Editors
Maria McKinney-Smith
Carol Layton
Kelly Gunzenhauser
Hank Rudisill
Erin Proctor
Kim Byerly

Art Directors
Pam Thayer
Alain Barsony
Penny Casto

Art Coordinator
J.J. Rudisill

Illustrators
Courtney Bunn
Mike Duggins
Erik Huffine
Kelly Johnson
David Lackey
Ray Lambert
Wayne Miller
Bill Neville
Betsy Peninger
Dez Perrotti
Britney Trivette
Julie Webb

Cover Design
Amber Kocher Crouch
Ray Lambert
J.J. Rudisill

Carson-Dellosa Publishing Company, Inc.

April

Table of Contents

APRIL TEACHER TIPS

Daily Surprise
Some students rarely earn treats or rewards in class, so every once in a while, give a reward just for fun! Ask a teacher who is not familiar with your class to choose a student's desk. Then, before school, post a picture of a smiley face on the door and place a lollipop, pencil, homework coupon, etc., in the desk of the lucky student. Explain to students that when they see the smiley face on the door, they should search their desks for the treat!

Eliminate Absent Papers
Help students keep up with missed assignments. Laminate a brightly-colored file folder. Write the name of the absent child on the front of the folder with an overhead pen and place the folder on her desk. Ask a child to place a copy of any assignments in the folder as they are passed out. When the student returns to school, she can take the papers home in the folder, then erase her name and return the folder to be used again.

Clean Transparencies
Eliminate the need to clean printed transparencies each year and also avoid getting messy marks from overhead pens on your hands or clothing. Project transparencies onto a chalkboard or dry erase board and write directly on the board instead of on the transparency.

Journal Grading
Rotate journals to cut down on grading time. Color-code student journals with colored dot stickers so 4-5 journals have red dots, 4-5 have orange, and so on. Collect a different color each week to grade, rotating in color order to remember which color is next.

Save Your Place
Students love to open their textbooks at exactly the right page. Give them special markers to help them do this every day and therefore eliminate long transition times. Give each student a self-stick note for each textbook. At the end of each lesson, have him flag the page for the next day's lesson before putting away his book.

No Mud
Keep your classroom floor clean and dry during April's rainy weather. Purchase a bath mat or small rug. Place two-sided tape on the back of the mat and press it to the floor just inside the classroom door. Hang a sign outside the classroom that reads *Please be neat and wipe your feet!*

April

Day-by-Day Calendar

1 *April Fool's Day* Have students write and illustrate their favorite jokes. Bind the pages together to make a class joke book.

2 *Hans Christian Anderson's Birthday* The famous children's author was born today in 1805. Bring in different versions of *The Emperor's New Clothes* and read them to the class.

3 *Washington Irving's Birthday* The author was born on this day in 1783. Celebrate by reading *Rip Van Winkle*.

4 *Reading a Road Map Week* is April 4-10. Bring in road maps of your town and divide the class into teams. Give a common starting point and ask the class to provide directions to a street, store, neighborhood, etc.

5 *Booker T. Washington's Birthday* Born into slavery, he founded Tuskegee Institute. Have students research his life to find out why education was so important to him.

6 The *first modern Olympics* were *held* today in Athens, Greece in 1896. Create sporting events centered around classroom subjects, such as a Long Distance Spelling Bee, High Jump Math Facts, or Triathlon Trivia.

7 *World Health Day* Have students keep a journal titled *A Healthy Me* that includes all the healthy things they do for themselves, such as eating healthy meals, exercising, and getting plenty of sleep.

8 *Keep America Beautiful Month* Have students pick up trash and recyclables around school and dispose of them properly.

9 *ZAM! Zoo and Aquarium Month* Create a ZAM! bulletin board. Ask students to bring in or draw pictures of animals found in zoos or aquariums.

10 *National Humor Month* Ask students to bring in things from home that make them laugh—books, toys, pictures, etc. Have a humorous *Show and Tell*!

11 The *first barber shop quartet organization* was *established* on this day in Tulsa, Oklahoma in 1938. Explain that a barbershop quartet is a singing group made up of four singers. Create a large cut-out of the numeral four and let students create collages of other things that come in fours.

12 The *first man went into space* on this day in 1961. His name was Yuri Gagarin and he was a Soviet cosmonaut. Ask students what they would pack in their suitcases if they were going into space.

13 *Thomas Jefferson's Birthday* The third president of the United States was born today in 1743. Jefferson's face can be found on the nickel and the two-dollar bill. Ask how many nickels are in a quarter and how many two-dollar bills are in twenty dollars.

14 *Anne Sullivan's Birthday* The teacher was born on this day in 1866. Teach the importance of perseverance by sharing the story of Anne Sullivan and Helen Keller.

15 *Leonardo da Vinci's Birthday* He was born today in 1452. Da Vinci was both a scientist and an artist. Have students draw their own inventions that would help make a job they do easier.

16 *Wilbur Wright's Birthday* The aviation pioneer was born today in 1867. Have students research facts about airplanes.

17 The *first Hershey® bar* was *sold* today in 1895. Have students pretend they bought the first Hershey® bar and write paragraphs describing the taste to others.

18 *Paul Revere's ride took place* today in 1775. During the Revolutionary War, he was responsible for warning Americans that the British were coming. In honor of Revere's important message, have students sit in a circle. Start a secret message around the circle. Have the last student say the message out loud.

19 *School Library Media Month* Have students make bookmarks to donate to the media center at your school.

20 *National Youth Sports Safety Month* Have students research safety tips for different sports. Then, have children make the facts into posters to display on a bulletin board.

21 *Friedrich Froebel's Birthday* The father of kindergartens was born today in 1782. He created the kindergarten setting we know today. Read *Mrs. Bindergarten Gets Ready for Kindergarten* to celebrate.

22 *National Playground Safety Day* Brainstorm a list of playground safety rules. Create a Playground Safety booklet to share with other classes.

23 *Sergei Sergeivitch Prokofiev's Birthday* The Russian composer was born today in 1891. He is famous for his musical fairy tale *Peter and the Wolf*. Bring in the musical version for students to enjoy.

24 *Maurice Sendak completed* the *first draft of Where the Wild Things Are* today in 1963. Share this story with the class. Have students draw pictures of what they would find if they visited where the wild things are.

25 *Math Education Month* Take today's date and turn it into amazing math problems. Give each child paper and see how many ways they can show the number 25.

26 *John James Audubon's Birthday* The bird lover was born today in 1785. Take the class outside to watch birds. Ask students to record the birds' activities in journals.

27 *Recycling Month* Have students research materials that are recyclable. Have them draw pictures of things that are made with these materials.

28 *National Lawn and Garden Month* Have students create an imaginary packet of seeds for a new kind of flower or plant that will do something spectacular.

29 The *zipper* was *patented* today in 1913. Ask students to count all the zippers in the classroom. Tell them not to forget zippers on pencil pouches, notebooks, and book bags.

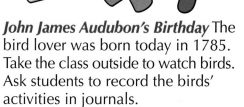

30 *National Honesty Day* Brainstorm a list of benefits of being honest. Have each student illustrate one of these benefits. Display the drawings on a bulletin board titled ____*Graders are Great, Honestly!*

5

Sunday	Monday	Tuesday	Wednesday	Thursday	Friday	Saturday

April

April Gazette

Teacher _____ Date _____

IN THE NEWS

WHAT'S COMING UP

TAKE NOTE

KID'S CORNER

Unscramble these words.

1. inary _____

2. bmlealur _____

3. tmors _____

4. udolcs _____

5. niawbor _____

Answers: 1. rainy 2. umbrella 3. storm 4. clouds 5. rainbow

© Carson-Dellosa CD-2097

7

Celebrate April!

Dear Family Members,
Here are a few quick-and-easy activities to help you and your child celebrate special days throughout the month of April.

April is *Zoo and Aquarium Month*

- Visit a local zoo or aquarium with your child. Take pictures during the outing and compile the photos into a scrapbook. Encourage your child to draw or write about the animals he or she saw and include the descriptions with the photos.

April is *National Lawn and Garden Month*

- Plant a special garden with your child and watch it, and your child's excitement, bloom! Dig a small flower bed in your yard, or fill a large container (with a drainage hole) with soil. Visit a garden center with your child and choose easy-to-grow vegetable or flower seeds. Plant the seeds together and encourage your child to water and maintain the garden, observing and enjoying it grow.

Reading a Road Map Week is April 4-10

- Road trip! Plan a day trip with your child using a road map. Use a highlighter to trace the route you will take. Have your child read the map to navigate the journey.

Leonardo da Vinci's Birthday is April 15

- Celebrate this famous scientist and painter of the Mona Lisa. Visit a library or a bookstore with your child and look at some of da Vinci's paintings and drawings. At home, paint pictures with your child. Frame the works of art with colorful construction paper and display them on the refrigerator or on a wall.

First Hershey®'s bar was sold on April 17

- Commemorate this delicious date in 1895 with s'mores!
  - 2 Hershey®'s bars
  - 4 marshmallows
  - 8 graham cracker squares

Break each Hershey®'s bar in half and stack each half on top of a graham cracker. Toast the marshmallows carefully over a flame on a fork. (Use a pot holder to hold the fork.) Place a toasted marshmallow on top of the graham cracker and chocolate and top with another graham cracker. Press down on the top cracker and let the heat of the marshmallow partially melt the chocolate bar, then enjoy! Makes four s'mores.

John James Audubon's Birthday is April 26

- This naturalist and artist painted many realistic pictures of wild birds. Go bird watching with your child, and take binoculars along, if they are available. Count the number of birds you see and sketch them, if desired. Check out a field guide of wild birds from the library and try to identify the birds you see.

Read In April!

Dear Family Members,
Here are some books to share with your child to enhance the enjoyment of reading in April.

 I Bought a Baby Chicken by Kelly Milner Halls
- *A little girl buys a baby chicken at the general store, inspiring each family member to also buy baby chicks. Each buys one more than the last until the family has over 50 chicks!*
- After reading the story, challenge your child to count the total number of chicks the family buys.

 Cat and Mouse in the Rain by Tomek Bogacki
- *Cat and Mouse are disappointed when they meet in the meadow only to discover it's raining.*
- Read the story and let your child tell about a rainy day adventure with a friend.

 The Egg Tree by Katherine Milhous
- *A Caldecott Medal book about an Easter egg hunt and the rediscovery of an Egg Tree tradition.*
- Start an Egg Tree Tradition with your child. Make a small hole with a pin in each end of an egg and blow out the insides. Paint or dye the egg and tie a ribbon in the top. Hang the decorated eggs on a branch affixed in plaster. (Fill a large plant pot 3/4 full with plaster of paris. Place a tree branch in the center and let the plaster harden.)

 Chicken Sunday by Patricia Polacco
- *Children make and sell traditional Pysanky eggs to buy a special Easter hat.*
- Make a variation of Pysanky eggs. Draw designs on hard-boiled eggs with a white crayon. Dye the eggs in a mixture of a few drops food coloring, one teaspoon white vinegar, and 1/2 cup warm water. Once dry, add an additional crayon design and dip the eggs in another color.

 Miz Fannie Mae's Fine New Easter Hat by Melissa Milich
- *Tandy and her Daddy buy Mama a fancy Easter hat with flowers and fruit and four specked eggs.*
- Let your child decorate a special Easter hat. Glue a paper bowl on top of a paper plate to make the base. Then, let your child color or paint it and glue on flowers, twigs, etc.

 Dora's Eggs by Julie Sykes
- *Dora is proud of her eggs until she sees the other farm animals with their cute and cuddly babies. In comparison, her eggs do not seem as wonderful—until they finally hatch.*
- Help your child draw pictures of different animals on the fronts of index cards and their babies on the backs. Place the cards face down on a table and play a memory matching game.

 ***Rain Song*** by Lezlie Evans
- *Simple rhyming verse tells about two girls' excitement as a thunderstorm approaches.*
- Read the story together with your child. After you read the narrative aloud, let your child read the rain sounds.

Reading Makes Me Hoppy

Name

Signed

Date

© Carson-Dellosa CD-2097

turned in
a Shower of Good Work

Signed

Date

© Carson-Dellosa CD-2097

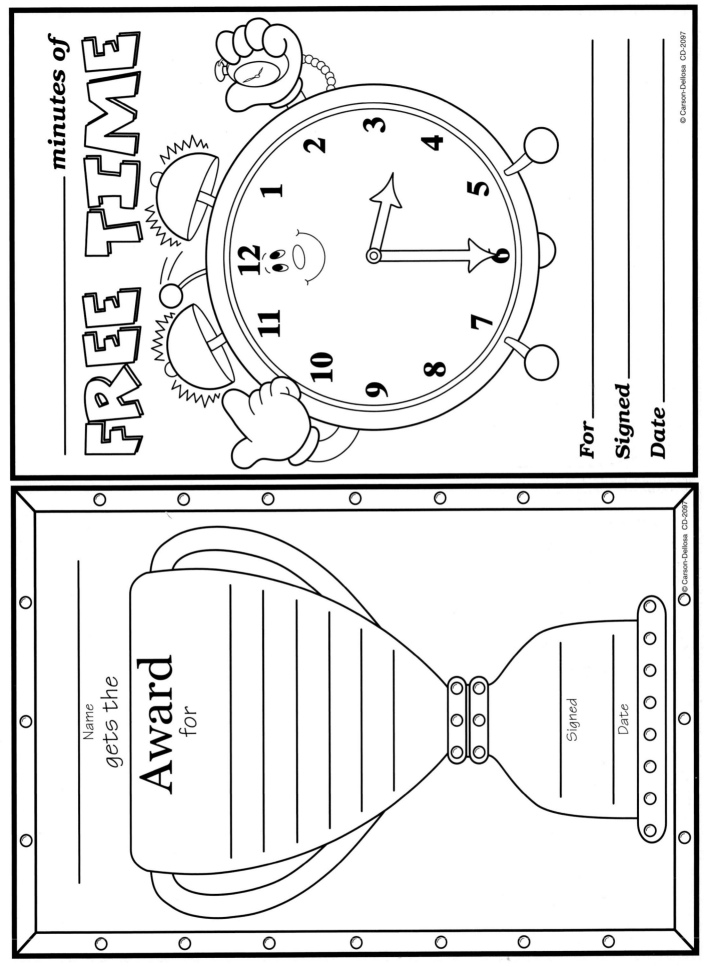

_____ minutes of

FREE TIME

For _____
Signed _____
Date _____

© Carson-Dellosa CD-2097

_____
Name
gets the

Award
for

_____

Signed _____
Date _____

© Carson-Dellosa CD-2097

11

April showers may bring May flowers, but rainy days can give students the blues. Wash away the boredom with writing activities that focus on spring, Easter, and the future.

WANTED

The Easter Bunny has quit his job and a new bunny must be hired immediately! Challenge students to write descriptive classified ads for the job of Easter Bunny. For example, *Needed: one large bunny, long ears, and a twitching pink nose; must own large basket with handle and have own egg source; a flair for color is a plus.* Display the students' ads on a bulletin board covered with classified pages of newsprint. Title the display *Needed Immediately: One Easter Bunny!*

Word Bank Words

thunder	showers
Easter	rain
bunny	umbrella
chicks	puddle
eggs	cloud
recycle	basket
environment	mud
grass	Earth

Guess the Word

Students spell it out to win this guessing game! Choose one student to come to the front of the class. Have her secretly write one of the week's spelling words on a piece of paper. Then, call on other students to guess the word she wrote. Have them ask, "Is the word ____?," spelling the word they guess. The student at the front must reply either "yes" or "no, the word is (or is not) ____," spelling the word guessed. The student who correctly guesses and spells the secret word comes to the front of the class to choose the next secret word.

Welcome to the World

Celebrate the new births of spring! Spring is in the air and baby animals are being born. Have each student choose a baby animal and write it a letter, welcoming it into the world. Students can describe all the things the animal will do and see, warn it of dangers, and wish it good luck.

Future Earth

Practice writing in the "future tense." Prompt students to envision the future of our planet. Have them write stories about what the Earth will be like hundreds of years from now. Will everything run on solar energy? Will the air be polluted? What new forms of transportation will we use? Encourage students to use their imaginations and suggest new inventions, technology, etc., that might exist in the future.

This is Your Life

Don't touch that dial! What would it be like to have your life portrayed on television? Let each child choose a memorable, funny, or exciting event in his life to write about, but in television script form. Have students include dialog for each character, narration, stage directions, etc. If desired, let several children direct classmates in acting out their scripts.

A Story of Misstakes

Students learn from their mistakes in this writing and editing exercise. Have children compose a paragraph with as many mistakes as possible. Ask them to spell words wrong, use incorrect words, and misuse punctuation and capitalization. Have them count the mistakes and write the number at the top of the page. Have students exchange papers and edit. Challenge each child to find any mistakes that the original writer missed!

It's Raining Poetry

Have your class singing in the rain with this sensory writing exercise. Ask students to close their eyes and imagine a rainstorm. If desired, play a recording of rain. Give each child a raindrop pattern (page 74) copied on blue paper. On the patterns, have students write poems about rain. Let students describe the way rain sounds, looks, smells, tastes, and feels. Display the raindrops together on a bulletin board or as a mobile falling from a large cloud.

Spring Rules!

Let students lay down the laws about spring! Ask them to think about ways they enjoy a spring day. Then, in their journals, have them write 4-5 rules for enjoying a spring day, such as *you must stomp in every puddle you see* or *keep your eyes and ears open*.

Bulletin Board Ideas

Show students what it takes to be a "good egg"! Make a large paper basket, staple it to the bulletin board and fill with crumpled tissue paper. Add tissue paper flowers with pipe cleaner stems. Provide each student with two egg patterns (page 29). Have her decorate one, and write an example of good behavior on the other. Cut the decorated egg in half in a zigzag line, then tape the halves to the good behavior egg at the top and bottom. Tape the eggs to the board and allow students to open the flaps and see what it takes to be a "good egg." Use during the *Easter is on its Way* chapter (pages 20-31).

Students will hop at the chance to display their Easter prose and poems on this bulletin board. Decorate copies of the egg pattern (page 29) to use as a border. Construct a bunny by drawing or decorating the face on a paper plate. Cut a large construction paper circle for the body, two small circles for hands, two small ovals for feet, and two large ovals for ears. Use cotton balls for tails and clouds. Have students write their Easter poems or stories on the bunnies' bodies. Use this bulletin board during the *Easter is on its Way!* chapter (pages 20-31).

14

SNUGGLE UP TO MOTHER
Match the picture and name of each mother to the correct baby

seal — pup
beaver — kitten
kit
opossum — baby
foal
deer — fawn
whale — calf
joey
whelp
koala — joey
bear — cub
Patterns and Names

Make a snuggly baby animal quilt! Staple pastel paper rectangles to a bulletin board. Draw dotted lines or attach yarn between the rectangles to represent stitches and ties. Attach labeled copies of the baby animal patterns (pages 36-40) to the board. Place labels and copies of the mother animal patterns (pages 36-40) in an envelope. Let students choose the correct mother name and picture to attach to the board, matching each mother to her baby. Use this bulletin board during your study of *Animals and Their Babies* chapter (pages 32-40).

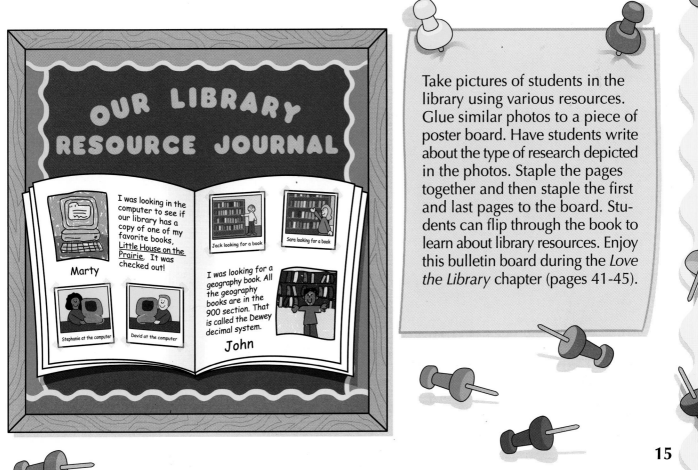

OUR LIBRARY RESOURCE JOURNAL

Marty — I was looking in the computer to see if our library has a copy of one of my favorite books, Little House on the Prairie. It was checked out!

Stephanie at the computer

David at the computer

Jack looking for a book

Sara looking for a book

John — I was looking for a geography book. All the geography books are in the 900 section. That is called the Dewey decimal system.

Take pictures of students in the library using various resources. Glue similar photos to a piece of poster board. Have students write about the type of research depicted in the photos. Staple the pages together and then staple the first and last pages to the board. Students can flip through the book to learn about library resources. Enjoy this bulletin board during the *Love the Library* chapter (pages 41-45).

15

This bulletin board provides hands-on practice in money skills. Cover a board with colorful paper and borders. Attach an enlarged copy of the purse pattern (page 50) and copies of the coin patterns (page 50) made on brown or gray paper. Attach the coins to the board with push pins. In the center of the purse, attach a money word problem, and allow students to solve the problem by attaching the correct coin combination to the purse. Change the word problem daily or weekly. This complements the *Catch on to Coins* chapter (pages 46-50).

I bought a drink for 79¢. I paid with a dollar bill. What would my change be?

soda bottles → carpets

paper → more paper

cans → grocery carts

milk jugs → hair combs

Help students understand what can and cannot be recycled with this bulletin board. Divide the board into three sections and label as shown above. Create the trash can and the recycling symbol from construction paper. Attach magazine cut-outs of various items in the center section. Have students move the items that cannot be recycled to the "trash" section. Move the items that can be recycled to the "treasure" section and label them with what they could be recycled into. Use this interactive bulletin board during your study of *Celebrate Earth Day* (pages 55-64).

Encourage students to think literally about cleaning the earth. Construct a tub shape from construction paper. Place an enlarged copy of the Earth pattern (page 63) in the tub. Accent the board with bubbles cut from plastic wrap. Have students write paragraphs on ways to keep the Earth clean. Staple the papers to colorful construction paper and attach to the board. Display this bulletin board during your study of *Celebrate Earth Day* (pages 55-64).

Let students discover the many reasons for trees! Cover the bottom of the bulletin board with green paper cut to resemble grass. Give students large sections of butcher paper and have them sponge paint it in tree colors, then cut out tree shapes. Attach the trees to trunks cut from brown paper. Title the board *I Would Plant a Tree Because . . .* and have students finish the sentence by writing on their trees. Use this bulletin board during your study of *Arbor Day* (pages 65-67).

Use this colorful and informative bulletin board to enhance the *It's Raining, It's Pouring* chapter (pages 68-74). Cover a bulletin board with light blue paper, and add strips of blue scalloped border at the bottom to represent the ocean. The sun and cloud can be made from paper, the rain from blue yarn, and the water vapor from twisted plastic wrap. Label each part of the water cycle and place arrows to show the direction of the cycle. Let students take turns explaining the water cycle in their own words.

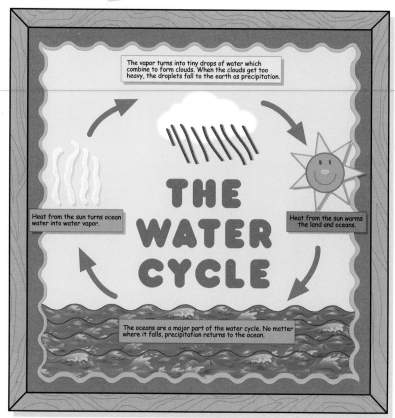

Great ideas "inhabit" this bulletin board. Divide the bulletin board into four sections and the class into four groups. Assign each group a habitat and a section of the board. Have each group illustrate its habitat and cut out or draw animals and plants that live in that habitat. Use this bulletin board to show what students have learned during your study of *Wildlife* (pages 75-84).

Create a bar graph of the class's favorite habitats. Have each child pick an animal they would most like to be and research specifically where in its habitat it lives. Students can draw their animals on color-coded paper to represent the habitat and write where the animal lives. Graph the students' work to find out which habitat is most popular. Display this bulletin board during your study of the *Wildlife* chapter (pages 75-84).

Each week during poetry month, compose a poem or choose a favorite poem to display. Write the poem on a large sheet of paper. Curl the ends of the paper to look like a scroll, then tape the rolled edges. Have students write or illustrate responses to the poem and post them beside the poem. This bulletin board enhances activities during *National Poetry Month* (pages 85-92).

Easter is on its way!

As new life springs from the Earth, Christians celebrate the death and resurrection of Jesus Christ. The holiday has its roots in the Jewish Passover which commemorates Israel's deliverance from slavery in Egypt. The crucifixion of Jesus led first century Christians (many of whom were Jewish) to celebrate the resurrection of Jesus as part of the Passover. The Friday preceding Easter is now known as Good Friday and marks Jesus' crucifixion. The sunrise services held in graveyards on Easter Sunday morning celebrate the resurrection and the promise of eternal life. Christians sometimes greet each other on this day with the proclamation, "Christ the Lord is risen!" and the refrain, "Christ the Lord is risen, indeed!" Enhance children's celebration of the Easter season with these attractive and fun crafts.

Did You Know?

- The Easter Bunny started as a legend in Germany. During a famine, a woman dyed Easter eggs for her children and hid them in a nest. When the children found the eggs, a rabbit leapt away. The story spread that the rabbit had delivered the eggs.
- Eggs were dyed and given as gifts as early as the Middle Ages.
- The first Easter bunny treats were made in the early 1800s in Germany.

Literature Selections

The Bird's Gift: A Ukrainian Easter Story by Eric A. Kimmel: Holiday House, 1999. (Picture book, 32 pg.) A young girl rallies to save birds who are buried in the snow.

Humbug Rabbit by Lorna Balian: Humbug Books, 1987. (Picture book, 32 pg.) Papa rabbit's children think he is the Easter bunny even though he denies it.

The Bunny Who Found Easter by Charlotte Zoltow: Houghton Mifflin, 1998. (Picture book, 32 pg.) Classic tale of a bunny searching for Easter.

Easter Wreaths

These wreaths are sure to get students ready for Easter! Give each student a ring of cardboard or poster board and some Easter grass. Have students glue the grass around the rings. Duplicate reduced egg patterns (page 29) for students to decorate, cut out, and glue to the wreaths. Give each student a bow pattern (page 30) to color and attach to the wreath as a finishing touch. Display the Easter wreaths on your classroom door as a reminder of the holiday.

Egg Roll

United States President Rutherford B. Hayes began the traditional White House Easter egg roll in 1878. He gave specific orders to allow any child onto the lawn who wanted to participate. Successive presidents have continued this tradition which is held on the south lawn. Let students participate in a class Easter egg roll. Place masking tape on the floor of the classroom to indicate start and finish lines. Let 4 or 5 students participate in each race. Give each racer a plastic Easter egg to place at the starting line. Tell students that the object of the game is to roll the egg with a spoon to the finish line. The first student to roll an egg across the line wins. Continue the game until everyone has a chance to race. Reward the players with jelly beans or Easter chocolates.

Easter Lilies

Easter is in bloom! The traditional flower of Easter is the Easter lily. Create a wall or bulletin board display featuring a pot of these flowers. Draw a large flower pot with stems and leaves on the bulletin board. Give each student one egg carton cup, five petal patterns (page 30), orange construction paper, and white paint. Have students paint their egg carton cups white. After the cups have dried, let students glue the petals to the insides of the cups and carefully curl back the tips of the petals. Have students cut three thin strips of orange construction paper to glue inside the flowers as pistils. Let each student glue his Easter lily to a stem on the bulletin board to complete the Easter display.

Easter Bonnets

Don some Easter spirit with these bonnets! Give each student a paper plate and a colorful plastic bowl. Place the bowl on the bottom of the plate and trace its outline. Cut out the center of the plate. Glue the bowl to the bottom of the plate, creating a hat shape. After the plates have dried, let students draw and cut out flowers, Easter candies, etc., to glue to their bonnets. Attach a wide streamer to each side of the plate rim. Let students wear the bonnets by loosely tying the streamers under their chins.

21

Papier Mâché Eggs

These unique Easter eggs will add a colorful touch to your classroom. Make a batch of papier mâché using the recipe below and pour into a shallow pan. Give each student a small balloon that has been blown up. Have students dip strips of newspaper into the papier mâché and place them on the balloons. Cover the balloons entirely with newspaper and let dry overnight. Add a second layer of papier mâché after the first has dried completely. Let students paint the dried balloons to look like Easter eggs. Spray each balloon with shellac. Poke two small holes in the top of each egg and thread with nylon string to hang the eggs from the *Easter Tree* (below).

Papier Mâché
2 parts water
1 part flour
Mix ingredients until thin.

Easter Tree

Make a holiday tree to display students' Easter decorations. Fill a large flower pot ³/₄ full with plaster of paris. Place a tree branch in the center and let the plaster harden. Place the tree in a central location and let students hang the *Papier Mâché Eggs* (above) and other Easter crafts from the branch.

Mosaic Egg Necklaces

Turn eggshells into colorful works of art! Prepare for the activity by washing several eggshells thoroughly. Crush the shells with a spoon until they are in small pieces. Fill several containers with water, add a few drops of food coloring to each, and let the shells soak in the mixtures. Allow the shells to dry, then put them in plastic bags. In class, copy an egg pattern (page 29) on tagboard for each student. Punch a hole in the top of each pattern. Thread a length of string or yarn through the hole long enough to fit around a student's neck. Provide students with dyed eggshells. Children can brush the patterns with white glue and cover completely with the egg shells. When the glue is dry, let students wear their eggs as necklaces.

22

Ukranian Easter Eggs

Design your own Easter eggs! Ukrainian Easter eggs are dyed using a process called *pysanky*. A dye-resistant material is put on the eggs in special designs. When the eggs are dyed, the dye-resistant material protects that part of the shell from the dye. Let students dye eggs using this process. Give each student a hard-boiled egg and a white crayon. Have students draw designs on the eggs using the crayons. Then, provide several different colors of dye (boil water with a few drops of food coloring; add one teaspoon of white vinegar and let cool). Let students dip their eggs in the dye with tongs. If desired, students may dip their eggs in more than one color.

"Hoppy" Easter Cards

Some "bunny" will feel special receiving this cute card! Give each student an enlarged copy of the egg pattern (page 29) to trace on construction paper and cut out. Decorate the egg shape like a rabbit's face using wiggly eyes, crayons, and a pink pom-pom for the nose. Next, have students trace each of their hands on construction paper, cut them out, and glue them to the tops of the eggs to create bunny ears. Have students write Easter messages on the ears and take the cards home to share.

What Would You Give the Easter Bunny?

At this time of year, the Easter bunny spends a lot of time giving. What do students think would be the perfect gift for him to receive? Cut a large bunny face and ears from construction paper and post it on the bulletin board. Then, give each student a basket pattern (page 31) and an egg pattern (page 29) to decorate. On the eggs, have students write what gifts they would give the Easter bunny. Cut slits near the tops of the baskets and slide the eggs into the slits. To read what gifts are in store for the Easter bunny, gently pull each egg out of the basket. Post the baskets on a bulletin board and title it *Thank You, Easter Bunny!*

Chocolate Bunnies

Make chocolate bunnies that will last long after Easter has passed! Give each student two chocolate bunny patterns (page 29) to color brown. Provide small candy buttons for students to glue to their bunnies for eyes. Staple the two patterns together except for the head. Have students stuff the bunnies with cotton and add sprinkles of cocoa for a chocolate scent. Then, staple the bunnies closed. If desired, give each student a piece of cellophane in which to wrap her bunny and tie the cellophane with ribbon at the top. Have students attach gift cards with special Easter messages and take the bunnies home as gifts for friends or family members.

Hang on to Your Bunnies!

Students will want to "hang" onto these adorable bunnies! Give each student a spindle clothespin, construction paper, wiggly eyes, white paint, a pom-pom, and a paint brush. Let students paint the clothespins white. When the clothespins have dried, turn them so the round knob is at the bottom and the two arms are at the top, representing bunny ears. Glue wiggly eyes and a pink pom-pom nose to the round knob. Attach a piece of magnetic tape to the back of the clothespin to create a magnet.

Easter Bunny Plates

Step up to the plate with this Easter bunny craft! Give each student two paper plates and have her cut one in half. Then, have her glue the two halves, which represent bunny ears, to the top of the other plate. Give students jelly beans to glue on for eyes and noses, and licorice sticks to glue on as whiskers. Provide white construction paper and have students cut out two squares to glue on for teeth. Punch a hole in the top of each Easter bunny plate and hang them, back-to-back, from the ceiling.

24

"Egg"cellent Bunnies

These egg bunnies make great Easter centerpieces. Give each student a hard-boiled egg, a large marshmallow, construction paper, and markers. Have students cut a 2" strip of construction paper and tape the ends together to form stands for the eggs. Let students draw bunny feet on the fronts of the paper strips, and draw bunny faces on the eggs with markers. Next, have students glue marshmallows to the backs of the eggs for tails. Have students cut out bunny ears from construction paper and glue them to the tops of the eggs. Let students take home their bunny eggs to display as holiday decorations.

Be Bunnies

Follow your nose to fun! Let students make these bunny noses and ears in celebration of Easter. Mark a trail in the classroom on which "bunnies" can hop. Place plastic eggs filled with jelly beans at the end of the trail for a special surprise.

Noses

Provide each student with a cup from an egg carton, a pipe cleaner, a pink pom-pom, and an elastic band. Have students turn their egg carton cups upside down and glue the pom-pom to the top. Then, tell students to cut the pipe cleaner into six equal sections and poke them through the sides of the cups to make whiskers. Next, let students cut two squares from white construction paper and glue them to the rims of the cups for teeth. Finally, punch a hole on either side of the cup and tie the ends of an elastic band through each, making sure the band is wide enough to fit around each student's head.

Ears

Give each student a paper head band, poster board, and glue. Have students cut out ear shapes from the poster board, color them to look like bunny ears, and attach them to the head bands.

Jelly Bean Frames

Let students capture an Easter moment with these unique holiday frames! First, take an instant picture of each student wearing his bunny ears and noses from *Be Bunnies* (above). Then, provide each student with jelly beans, glue, crayons, markers, and one piece of poster board slightly larger than the photo. Have each student glue the photo to the center of the poster board, then decorate the edges by gluing on jelly beans. Fold a 2" x 2" piece of cardboard in half and glue one end to the back of the frame to create a stand for the picture.

25

A Batch of Hatching Chicks

Here a peep, there a peep, everywhere a peep-peep! Fill your classroom with hatching chicks! Copy the egg pattern (page 29) for each student. Have him cut the top half off in a zigzag shape. Next, have each student attach the top part of the egg to the rest of the pattern with a paper fastener. Provide yellow construction paper for students to draw and cut out chick shapes that are slightly smaller than the egg patterns, and glue them to the backs of the eggs. Have students write poems about Easter chicks on the fronts of the egg patterns. After the students have read the poems, they can "hatch" the chicks by pulling up the top parts of the eggs!

Peck, peck
I found my way out!
Peep, peep
Happy Easter!

Chick Decorations

These fuzzy chicks will warm students' hearts. Give each student an egg pattern (page 29), a wing pattern (page 30), poster board, yellow felt, glue, and markers. Have each student trace two egg patterns and two wing patterns on the poster board and cut them out, then trace an egg shape and two wing shapes on the felt and cut them out. Glue the felt shapes on top of the poster board shapes. Then, have each student cut the remaining poster board egg shape in a zigzag pattern and glue the bottom to the felt egg shape. Glue the wings to the sides of the chick, and decorate with markers. If desired, punch a tiny hole in the top of each chick, thread plastic filament through, and hang from the *Easter Tree* (page 22).

Festive Easter Baskets

Don't put all your eggs in one basket—unless it's this basket! Give each student two pieces of construction paper, tape, and ribbon. Have students fold each piece of construction paper lengthwise, tape the edges, then tape the two pieces together. Next, fold the construction paper strip lengthwise again and cut slits one inch apart along the main fold. Have students unfold the strips once and weave several pieces of ribbon through the slits. Tape the ends of the ribbon so they stay in place. Form the strip into a basket shape and tape closed. Have each student trace the bottom circle shape of the basket on another piece of construction paper, cut out the circle, and tape it to the bottom of her basket. Let students cut construction paper strips to make handles and tape one end of the strip to each side of their baskets. Finally, give students Easter grass to place in their baskets. Fill the baskets with paper eggs and display in a special place in the classroom.

Hot Cross Buns

Hot cross buns are usually available in bakeries during the Easter season. Make hot cross buns to enjoy as a class treat.

Bun Ingredients

$4\frac{1}{2}$ cups flour
$\frac{1}{3}$ cup granulated sugar
2 tablespoons quick rise yeast
1 teaspoon salt
2 teaspoons cinnamon
$\frac{1}{2}$ teaspoon nutmeg

2 cups warm water
$\frac{1}{4}$ cup melted butter
2 tablespoons milk
2 eggs, beaten
1 cup raisins (optional)

Icing Ingredients

$1\frac{1}{2}$ cups confectioner's sugar
1-2 tablespoons milk
$\frac{1}{2}$ teaspoon vanilla extract

Combine the flour, sugar, yeast, salt, cinnamon, and nutmeg. Add the water, butter, milk, then the eggs. Vigorously stir the batter with a wooden spoon. Add the raisins. Turn the dough onto a floured surface and knead until smooth and elastic. Cover the dough with a towel until it doubles in bulk. Punch down and knead until smooth. Roll into 24 balls and place on greased baking sheets. Cover and let rise in a warm place for 20-30 minutes. Bake at 350º for about 20 minutes or until brown. Cool completely. Stir the icing ingredients together until smooth and drizzle over the buns in a cross shape. Makes 24 hot cross buns.

Easter Basket Cupcakes

Create Easter fun with these tasty treats! Prepare a batch of cupcakes according to package directions. Provide frosting, jelly beans, and licorice sticks. Let students decorate the cupcakes with frosting. Place jelly beans on top of the cupcakes to represent eggs. Let each student stick each end of a licorice stick into the side of the cupcake, resembling a basket handle. Let students enjoy these yummy Easter baskets while they complete the Easter Egg Match worksheet (page 28).

27

Easter Egg Match

Draw lines to connect the eggs that are alike and then color the eggs.

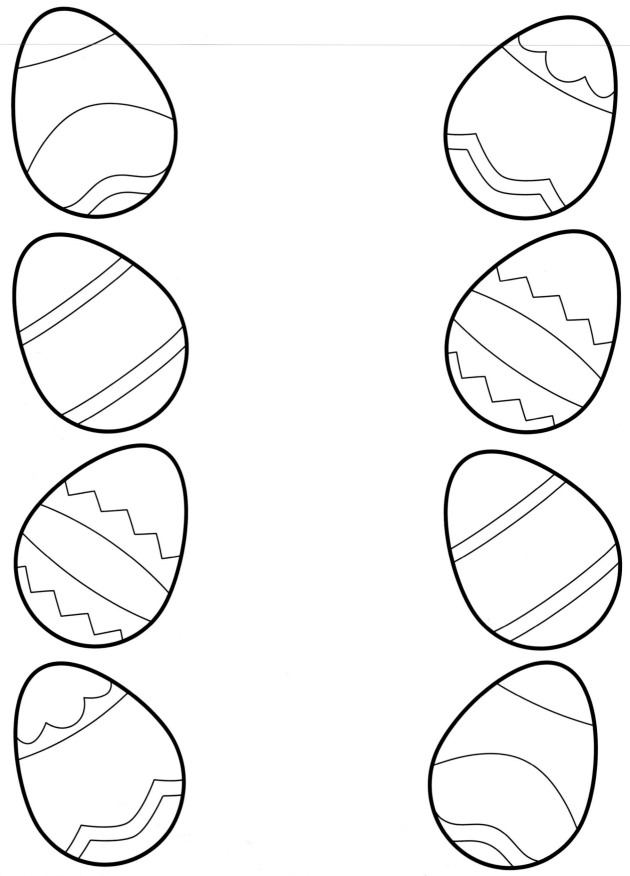

chocolate bunny

COPY and CUT

egg
(also use with bulletin
board idea, page 14)

29

© Carson-Dellosa CD-2097

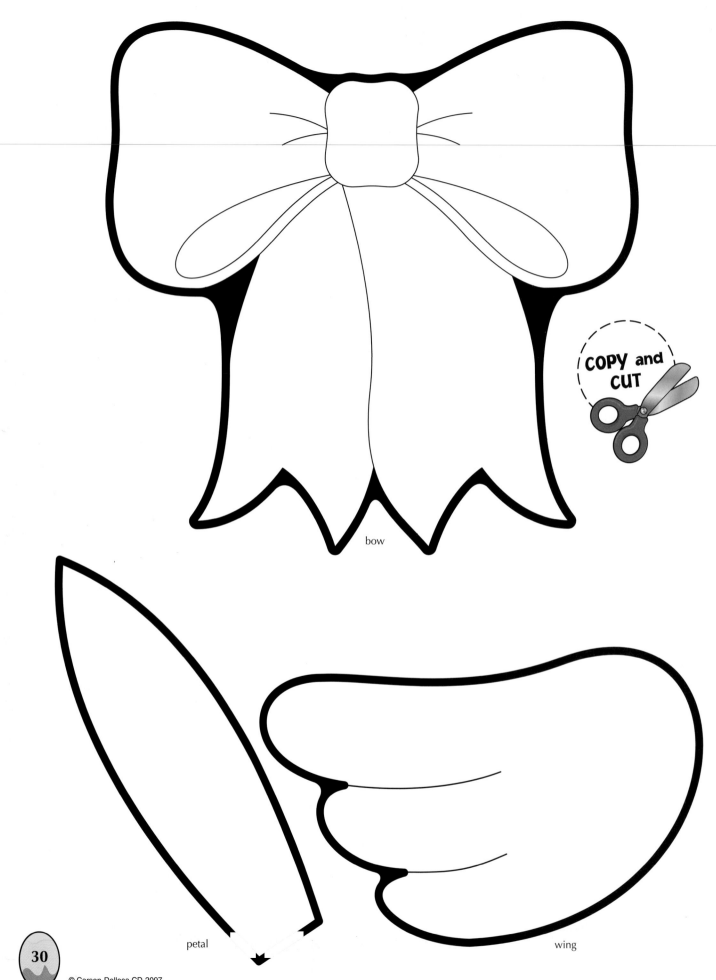

COPY and CUT

bow

petal

wing

basket

Animals and Their Babies

Whether they live in the wild, in a zoo, on a farm, or as pets, animal babies are always fascinating. Learn how different animals care for their young with the following activities.

Did You Know?

- Most mammals, such as monkeys, bears, and lions, care for their young and usually have two to four babies at a time.
- Animals that do not care for their young, such as frogs, turtles, and butterflies, lay hundreds or thousands of eggs at a time, since most will not survive.
- Most animals that hatch from eggs, such as amphibians, insects, and fish, never see their parents. After they hatch, they must survive on their own.

Literature Selections

Kangaroos Have Joeys by Philippa-Alys Browne: Atheneum Books for Young Readers, 1996. (Picture book, 32 pg.) The names of various animal babies are introduced through illustrations.

Animal Dads by Sneed B. Collard III: Houghton Mifflin Company, 2000. (Picture book, 32 pg.) An interesting look at how male animals help care for their young.

Dora's Eggs by Julie Sykes: Little Tiger Press, 1997. (Picture book, 32 pg.) As Dora the hen visits the farmyard animals and sees their babies, she wonders why she only has eggs.

My Baby Animal Album

Create adorable albums that feature baby animals, complete with pictures and keepsakes. As students learn about baby animals, give each child copies of the animal patterns (pages 36–40). Have each student glue one pattern to a sheet of paper and write about it. Let students make the animals textured with materials such as sandpaper, felt, cotton, and fabric scraps. For each animal, have students include the name of the mother, father, and baby, any special information, and a keepsake, such as baby footprints. Bind the pages to make an animal baby reference book for students.

mother's name- doe
father's name- buck
baby's name- fawn

My spots hide me from hungry predators.

footprint

Animal Baby Names

alligator–hatchling	elephant–calf	llama–cria	shark–pup
bat–pup	fish–fry	moose–calf	spider–spiderling
beaver–kitten	frog–tadpole	otter–whelp	squirrel–pup
camel–calf	goat–kid	owl–owlet	swan–cygnet
dragonfly–nymph	goose–gosling	penguin–chick	turkey–poult
duck–duckling	gorilla–infant	pigs–piglet	turtle–hatchling
eagles–eaglet	lion–cub	raccoon–cub	zebra–foal

egg

tadpole

frog

Hatched from an Egg

Which animals are hatched from eggs? Let students find out! Explain that all birds, turtles, alligators, and crocodiles hatch from eggs as well as most lizards, snakes, frogs, toads, and salamanders. Divide students into small groups and assign each a different animal. Let each group research the life stages of its animal from egg to adult. Then, provide sentence strips for each group to illustrate the life cycle of its animal. On the left end of the sentence strip, students should draw and label the egg. Have students illustrate and label the next stages, ending with the adult animal on the right end of the sentence strip. Post the completed life cycles on a wall or bulletin board for students to compare.

Babies in the Pouch

Marsupials, such as kangaroos, koalas, and opossums, keep their babies tucked away and protected in special pouches called *marsupia* (mar•SOO•pee•ah). Have students make pocket pictures filled with facts about these unique animals. Fold the bottom third of an 8½" x 14" piece of paper and tape the edges closed to create a pocket. Draw a kangaroo on the paper or use the kangaroo pattern (page 36), placing the pouch in the appropriate place. Make several copies of the kangaroo joey pattern (page 36) and have students cut them out. Let children research and write facts about marsupials on the patterns, then slide them into the pouches. Display the completed kangaroos on a bulletin board.

Where's my Mommy?

Help students match adult and baby animals. Divide the class into two teams. Write the names of several different mammals, reptiles, and birds in one column on a sheet of paper. Write the names of the animal babies beside the adult names in a second column. (See *Animal Baby Names*, page 32.) Cut apart the names in the first column and place them in a container. Have each child on one team choose an animal name. Then, cut apart the baby animal names in the second column, place them in a container, and let each child on the second team choose a name. Let the teams take turns asking each other *yes* or *no* questions, such as "Are you hatched from an egg?," "Do you live in a pouch?," or "Do you have feathers?" Let children use the answers to figure out which player has the matching animal parent or baby.

parents

babies

33

Is it Instinct or Learned?

All animals, including people, have instinctive behaviors. These are behaviors they are born knowing how to do. Challenge students to think of things they always knew how to do (instinctive) and things they were taught (learned). Provide reference books about animals and let students research animal behaviors. Have each student fold a sheet of paper into six sections by folding the paper into thirds, then in half vertically. In the first column, let each student draw and label an animal. In the two sections underneath, have her draw an instinctive behavior and a learned behavior. In the second column, let each student draw a picture of herself in the top section. Then, in the sections below, have her draw an instinctive behavior and a learned behavior. Allow students to share their illustrations with the class.

Goslings All in a Row

Many baby animals are born helpless and need adult animals to teach them how to walk, swim, find food, build homes, and escape from enemies. Baby geese, or goslings, follow the first moving thing they see after hatching and count on this "parent" to teach them the behaviors they need to learn. Let students act like geese or goslings with this game. Choose one student to be the goose. Have the other students stand in a line behind the goose and pretend to be goslings, imitating how the goose walks, jumps, skips, or hops around the room. Remind the goslings to stay in line behind the goose. Switch leaders by having the goose move to the end of the line, allowing the first gosling in line to become the goose.

Guess the Baby Animal

Which baby animal is your favorite? Let students choose, then create "hidden" pictures to share with classmates. Give each student a sheet of paper and instruct him to fold it in half from top to bottom. Open the paper and have each student draw a picture of a baby animal inside. Close the paper and cut a circle in the top sheet so only a small part of the picture underneath is visible. Have each student write clues to the animal's identity beside the circle. Let students trade papers and use the clues to guess each baby animal. Allow students to open the papers to check their answers.

What Every Baby Needs

What does a baby boy or girl have in common with a baby kangaroo? Explain that most mammals take care of their babies just as people do. Have students research how different animals care for their young, then think of similar things people do to care for their babies. **1.** Give each student a half sheet of paper and have her fold it in half from top to bottom. Staple the bottom edges of the paper closed. **2.** Cut a strip of paper 8½" long and 4" wide, slide it into the folded paper and have each student center the strip. **3.** Draw pencil lines where the edges of the folded paper meet the paper strip and write the word *Pull* at both ends of the paper strip. On the folded paper, have each student write something all babies need. **4.** Then, pull the strip on one side and illustrate and write about how an animal cares for its baby. **5.** Pull the other side of the strip and draw and write about how a person cares for her baby.

Animal Family Portraits

Just as there are different kinds of human families, there are also different kinds of animal families. Provide reference books and have students research animal families. Explain that male and female Canada geese, beavers, and dolphins each stay together and share the responsibility of feeding and protecting their young. Baby polar bears and deer are cared for by their mothers. Male emus and seahorses raise their young with little help from females. Wolves live in extended families that include grandparents, aunts, uncles, and cousins; all family members help raise younger animals. Allow each student to choose an animal family, cut out pictures of babies and caretakers from wildlife magazines, and glue the pictures to a large sheet of paper to create an animal family portrait. Have students label the portraits and decorate the frames with animal patterns, footprints, and habitats.

Shark and pup

When I Was a Baby

Your students will love seeing baby pictures of their classmates! Have students ask family members to share stories about them as babies. Let each student bring in a baby picture. On a bulletin board, post enlarged animal patterns (page 36-40), putting the adults with their babies. Then, allow children to write their baby stories, then post them on the bulletin board accompanied by their baby pictures. Let students guess who is who in each picture.

35

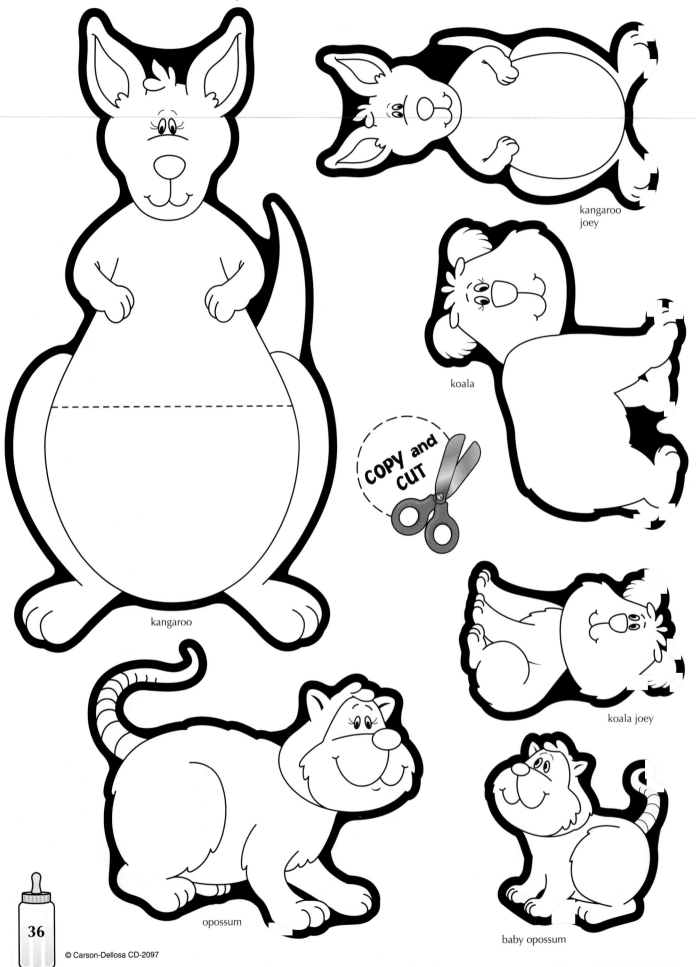

kangaroo joey

koala

COPY and CUT

kangaroo

koala joey

opossum

baby opossum

36

Animal patterns (also use with bulletin board idea, page 15)

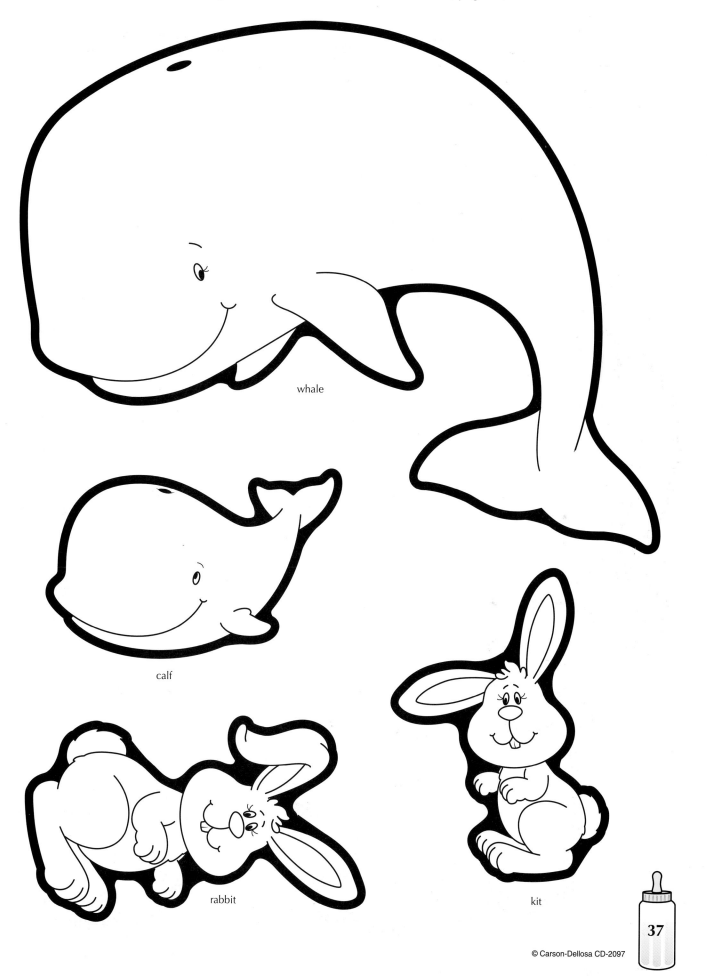

whale

calf

rabbit

kit

Animal patterns (also use with bulletin board idea, page 15)

bear

cub

COPY and CUT

foal

horse

© Carson-Dellosa CD-2097

Animal patterns (also use with bulletin board idea, page 15)

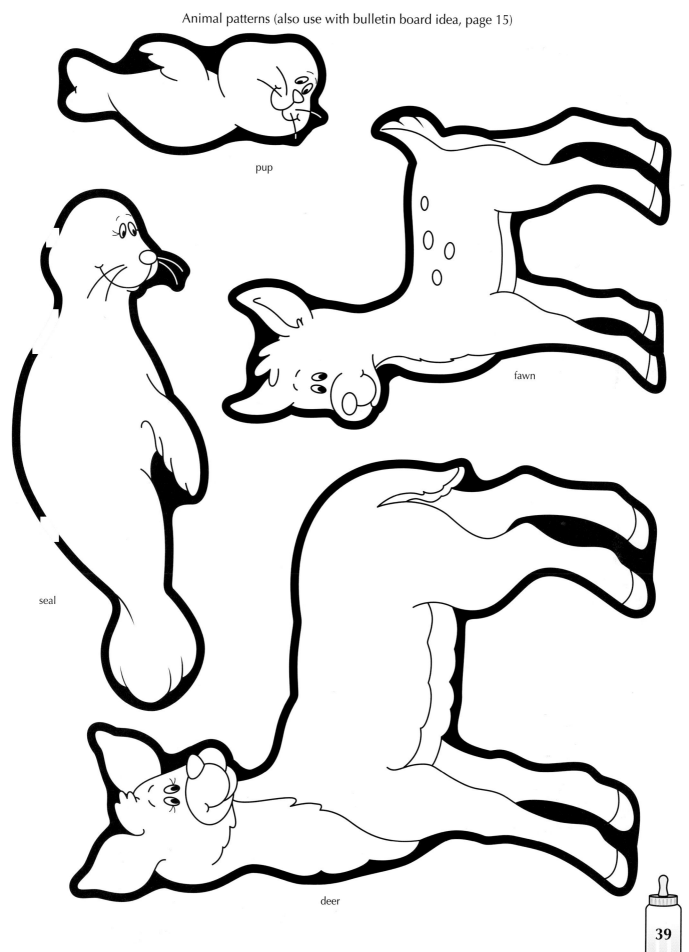

pup

fawn

seal

deer

Animal patterns (also use with bulletin board idea, page 15)

penguin

whelp

otter

COPY and CUT

chick

beaver

kitten

40

L♥ve the Library!

National Library Week is celebrated every April to encourage reading. Finding that special book will be easy for students as they learn to use library resources.

Did You Know?

Libraries have been around since 2700 B.C., when the Sumerians developed the first system of writing.

When the British army burned the Library of Congress in 1814, retired president Thomas Jefferson sold his personal library to the government to help rebuild the nation's library.

There is a library in California that houses only tools! People can use library cards to check out extension cords, drills, and hammers at no charge.

Literature Selections

The Library by Sarah Stewart: Farrar, Straus & Giroux, 1995. (Rhyming story book, 32 pg.) Elizabeth loves to read, but when her collection of books grows and grows, she must make a change in her life.

Stella Louella's Runaway Book by Lisa Campbell Ernst: Simon and Schuster, 1998. (Picture book, 40 pg.) A girl travels to find her misplaced library book.

The Library Dragon by Carmen Agra Deedy: Peachtree Publishers, 1994. (Picture book, 32 pg.) When a tyrannical dragon takes over as librarian, students help her realize that books are to be enjoyed, not just displayed.

Check This Out!

Create a mini-library that will have students rushing to read! Set up a special area of the classroom as the designated "library." Arrange books alphabetically or by subject. Tape copies of the book checkout card pattern (page 45) on index cards and file them alphabetically in a card box. Have students complete the card each time they take out a book or return it. Create a box for students to use when returning books. If desired, designate a specific amount of time students are allowed to keep each book. Assign a student librarian to re-shelve the books and let students volunteer to read favorite books aloud.

41

Star Reader!

Betsy

Bookmarks

No dog-eared pages in our books! Have students make bookmarks for the class mini-library (*Check This Out*, page 41). Copy several bookmark patterns (page 45) on heavy paper for each child. Punch holes where indicated and let students loop strands of yarn through the holes. Have children decorate them and then insert them into each of the class books.

Thanks for the Memories

Send the school librarian a thank-you book! Brainstorm a list of ways your librarian is important to the library and to students. Have each student write about and illustrate one reason in the form of a thank-you note to the librarian. Collect the completed pages and bind them into a thank-you book. Students can demonstrate skills the librarian has taught them by including a title page, table of contents, index, etc. Include a call number on the spine of the book and hide it in the stacks. Present the librarian with a mock card catalog card for the book, and let her find the book as a surprise.

It's Not Hard to Get a Card

Students will appreciate a library more when they become card-carrying patrons! Tour a local library and allow each child to apply for a library card. Explain how to use it and the responsibility that goes with having a card. Let each child record the title and author of a book he is not familiar with, or choose a favorite book and see if it is housed at that particular library. If possible, and with parent permission, allow students to check out children's books. Upon returning to the classroom, let each student decorate copies of the book label pattern (page 45). Children can take the labels home and tape them to the inside covers of their favorite personal books.

2 744 0378 4

PUBLIC LIBRARY

Amber Jones
Signature

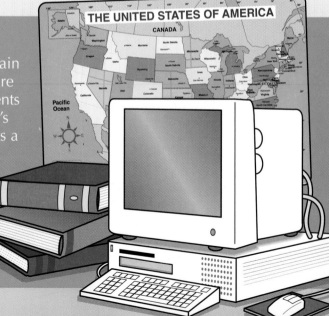

Specialized Libraries

Encourage students to think of a library as a place to gain access to many types of materials. Explain that there are libraries of tools, maps, and legal documents. Ask students what types of references would be needed in a doctor's office, a bakery, or on a farm. Brainstorm with students a list of different occupations and list on paper. Cut the paper into strips with one profession on each strip. Give each child a strip and have him brainstorm what types of materials would be needed in that specialized library. Let students invent book titles, book ideas, and draw pictures of the library.

How to Look for a Book

Turn the library into treasure island! Divide students into teams and give each team a different list of call numbers that will serve as "clues." Students should use knowledge of the Dewey Decimal System and the card catalog to find the books. Have students record the titles and when they have found the correct books, let them use the titles to discover what their prize will be. For example, their clues may take them to books about cows, milk, sugar, fruit and ice cream factories, and the prize would be ice cream. Stress that just like any good sleuth, students should remain quiet and work together as a team to uncover the prize.

945 = Italy
641.59 = Food
641.631 = Flour
641.6 = Tomato Sauce
647.95 = Pizza Parlors

Our Prize: Pizza Party!

Do We Know Dewey?

Students will forever remember Melvil Dewey and his system of library organization with this mnemonic device! Discuss the Dewey Decimal System's different categories and its purpose. Have students write a sentence incorporating the first letter of each category in order and illustrate it.

000: General Works
100: Psychology and Philosophy
200: Religion and Mythology
300: Social Sciences
400: Language
500: Natural Science
600: Applied Science
700: Fine Arts and Recreation
800: Literature
900: Geography and History

Give Penguins Red Slippers, Lizard Necklaces, And Furry Little Gorillas.

Categorizing Books

Fiction or nonfiction; that is the question! Explain that books in libraries are organized into these two categories. Discuss different genres and talk about which types of books are fiction and which are nonfiction. Have students write and illustrate a short story that is true or make-believe. Read the stories aloud to the class and let students vote whether it is fiction or fact. After the vote, let the author reveal the correct category. Divide the stories on a bulletin board under *Fiction* and *Nonfiction* headings along with book covers of other popular books.

43

Watch Dora cheer up when she gets her own babies to play with.

DORA'S EGGS
by Julie Sykes

It Pays to Advertise!

Students can make "best-sellers" of their favorite books! Have each child make a poster to publicize his favorite book from the school library. Provide students with white butcher paper in standard poster board dimensions (22" x 28"). Allow children to use markers, crayons, glitter, feathers, stencils, sand, etc., to bring their books to life. Students may choose to illustrate specific scenes, or imitate the covers of the books. Display the posters in the library and the hallway during Library Week to encourage students to visit the library.

Read to Me

Let students create their own "books-on-tape." Allow each student to choose her favorite book from the class library and read it aloud into a tape recorder. Encourage students to practice voice inflections to imitate characters and emotions. Classmates can assist with creating sound effects for the recordings. When the book is recorded, place it in a plastic storage bag with the tape. Make the tapes available for classes with children that cannot read. Check with the school librarian to determine if the tapes can be kept in a central area of the library. If desired, alternate the students weekly and have them record over the previous week's tapes.

Patricia Polacco
Chicken Sunday
Philomel Books
NY, NY 1992

EF
P

Summary: T...

EF
P

...or her ...inners, the ...and buy her

Egg Decoration
Chicken Sunday
Patricia Polacco
Philomel Books
NY, NY 1992

Summary: To thank old Eula for her wonderful Sunday Chicken dinners, the children ...rated eggs and buy her a bea...

Chicken Sunday
Patricia Polacco
Philomel Books
NY, NY 1992

EF
P

Summary: To thank old Eula for her wonderful Sunday Chicken dinners, the children sell decorated eggs and buy her a beautiful Easter hat.

SUPER Shoe Box

Introduce students to an age-old library resource, the card catalog! Pass out three large index cards to each student, as well as a book from the classroom library. Explain that each card is for a different method of organization used in a card catalog. On one side, students should record information pertaining to the book with the author's name as the heading. Have them repeat this with the remaining two cards, using the subject and the title as the headings. On the backs of each type, students can illustrate the author's picture or a scene from the book. (Explain that a real card catalog is not illustrated.) In a shoe box containing dividers, allow students to file their cards alphabetically by heading. Explain that a card catalog is a good way to obtain information about a book and that many libraries now have computerized catalogs which allow for electronic searches by author, subject, or title.

THIS BOOK BELONGS TO:

THIS BOOK BELONGS TO:

book labels

Star Reader!

bookmark

COPY and CUT

Book Title

Name

Date Signed Out

Date Returned

book checkout card

Catch on to Coins!

National Coin Week, the third week in April, is the perfect time to encourage students to become *numismatists* (new-MISS-ma-tists), or coin collectors!

DID YOU KNOW?

- The grooves on the edges of coins are called reeds. Coin designers put reeds on coins to differentiate coins of similar size.
- Ancient Chinese coins took the form of real or miniature tools such as spades, hoes, and knives. The smaller tokens had holes in them, making them easy to carry on a string.
- Booker T. Washington, Susan B. Anthony, Sacagawea, and Virginia Dare have appeared on U.S. coins.
- Not all coins are round. Coins may have four, eight, ten, or twelve sides, or may have wavy edges.

LITERATURE SELECTIONS

A Guide Book of United States Coins by R. S. Yeoman: Golden Books Pub. Co. (Adult), 2000. (Reference book, 336 pg.) The standard information and resource guide for coin collectors. Updated annually.
Coins and Currency by Brenda R. Lewis: Random House, 1993. (Hobby handbook, 80 pg.) Clear text and color illustrations introduce young readers to coins, coin history, and coin collecting.
My Rows and Piles of Coins by Tololwa M. Mollel: Clarion Books, 1999. (Storybook 32 pg.) A good-intentioned Tanzanian boy struggles to save enough money to buy a bicycle to help his parents.
The World of Coins and Coin Collecting by David L. Ganz: Bonus Books Inc., 1998. (Reference book, 250 pg.) Award-winning, illustrated guide to collecting, organizing, and displaying coins.

COIN RUBBINGS

Your students will discover that "change is good" when they make coin rubbings! Give each student an 11" x 17" paper and have him fold it in half four times to create a grid of 16 rectangles. Provide as many different coins as possible. To make rubbings, use one finger to keep the coin and paper from sliding, while applying even, moderate pressure with a crayon. Leave some rectangles blank for students to include foreign or other special coins they may have at home. Have students make rubbings of the front (obverse) and back (reverse) of each coin. Students can write the value and mint date under each rubbing.

25 cents 1998	25 cents 2003	$1.00 gold Sacajawea dollar	1 Cent Penny 1977
5 cents nickel 1962	25 cents 1999	Foreign Coin	25 cents 2000
Dime From Birthday 1993	10 cents 1988	1 cent 1978	25 cents 1999 Quarter from Grandpa
25 cents 1999	50 cents 1968	$1.00 Silver Dollar	25 cents 2001

COIN DETECTIVES

Fine-tune students' observation skills by letting them pretend to be coin detectives. Divide students into teams ("detective agencies") of 4-5 "agents" and tell them they have been hired to find as many similarities and differences among coins as possible. Give each "agency" a magnifying glass, a selection of coins, and a time limit for the exercise. Have groups examine the coins and list common elements such as size, shape, reeds, graphics, dates, mottos, and mint marks—the small single initial indicating whether a coin was minted in San Francisco (S), Denver (D), Philadelphia (P), or West Point, NY (W). Let each detective agency present its findings in an official report.

CLEAN COINS

Children will take a shine to this activity! Bring in used pennies and let children clean them. Tell students that most coins remain in circulation for about 25 years, and that handling and exposure eventually degrade the surfaces of coins. Mix $\frac{1}{2}$ cup lemon juice with 1 tablespoon salt in a plastic container. Provide old toothbrushes and let students polish the pennies. (Do not clean rare or valuable coins in this manner.)

MONEY AROUND THE WORLD

Teach students about the wide variety of currencies used by different countries. Post a world map on a bulletin board and assign each student a country. Ask each student to research the name(s) of the country's currency and make drawings of its coins. Have students create their reports on enlarged copies of the purse pattern (page 50) made on colorful paper. Post the reports around a bulletin board with the title *Money Around the World*.

Money Around the World

U.S. Coins
North America
Pacific Ocean
Atlantic Ocean
Europe
Italian Coins
Russian Coins
Asia
Chinese Coins
Pacific Ocean
Mexican Coins
Africa
South America
Kenyan Coins
Indian Coins
Indian Ocean
Australia
Pacific Ocean
Chilean Coins
Atlantic Ocean
Australian Coins
Antarctica

PURSE ESTIMATION

Fill students' "memory banks!" First, give each student the following items: a class roster, an enlarged copy of the purse pattern (page 50), and one or two copies of coin patterns (page 50). Have each student sign his purse on the front and glue any combination of coins to the back. Seat students in a circle. When you say "pass," each student should pass his purse to the classmate on his left. He should then look at the purse given to him, estimate the dollar amount shown, and writes that amount on the roster beside the name of the correct classmate. Give students 5-15 seconds to estimate each amount and write down an answer. Continue to say "pass" at regular intervals until each student has estimated each purse. Finally, have students write on the board or call out the amounts on their purses, and let other students check their estimates for accuracy.

PRICING PRODUCTS

Make an investment in students' economic know-how. Label classroom objects with price tags or create a price list on a bulletin board. Give each student several copies of the coin patterns (page 50) to cut out. Allow each student to use these coins as a budget for "buying" various classroom items. Use this activity to teach budgeting and money-counting skills.

COIN COMBINATIONS

Students will profit from this math and money exercise. Write different dollar amounts on slips of paper and place them in a hat. Divide the class into small groups and let each group pull a dollar amount from the hat. Challenge the groups to list all the combinations of coins that could make up that amount. Provide real coins or copies of the coin patterns (page 50) and have students cut out coins equivalent to the combinations and glue them to construction paper. Post the papers, labeled with each dollar amount, on a display titled *Making "Cents" of Money!*

HEADS OR TAILS?

Students will "flip" for this probability and graphing exercise. Ask students why they think people flip coins to make unbiased decisions and investigate with this activity. Pair students and give each pair a coin to toss. Have one student toss the coin 10 times while the other student records the results. Then, have the students switch roles and perform the exercise again. Instruct students to create pictographs of the results by making rubbings in columns depicting each "head" or "tail" result. On the board, total the results for the class and look for patterns. Have students make predictions for 20 or 30 coin tosses, and repeat the exercise to test their hypotheses. Ask students to draw conclusions about the fairness of tossing coins.

Catch on to Coins!

Queen Elizabeth I 1533-1603

Queen Elizabeth I
Elizabeth I, daughter of king Henry VIII, ruled England from 1558 to 1603. She presided over England's victory over the Spanish Armada in 1588, and helped establish stability for English religious and life. The colony (later, state) was named for her. She never married, though she had lots of offers.

Booker T. Washington 1856-1915

FAMOUS FIGURES

Coins can provide great history lessons! Tell students that for thousands of years, important people have been immortalized on coins. Give students a list of historic figures who have appeared on coins, then let them choose one to learn more about. Suggest Cleopatra, Julius Caesar, Ferdinand and Isabella of Spain, Isaac Newton, Ben Franklin, etc. Consult *Did You Know?* (page 46) for more historical figures. Have students cut out large paper "coins," write a biography of the person on one side, and draw a portrait of the person on the other. Organize the biographies by location or era and create mobiles to suspend them from the ceiling so students can read and learn from their classmates' work.

CLASS COMMEMORATION BOOK

Create a classroom book of commemorative coins! Have students think of important people, places, and events in their lives. Give each child a piece of paper and have him design, color, and cut out a two-sided commemorative coin to honor the special person, place, or event. Use clear tape to secure each coin in a sheet protector, and compile the class coins in a three-ring binder. If desired, let students include written descriptions of the coins. Inform students that Yellowstone National Park, the 200th anniversary of the United States, and Robert F. Kennedy have all been honored on commemorative coins.

My Teacher — Mr. Alexander

Number One Mom

LETTERS TO THE MINT

Polish your students' letter writing skills to mint condition by having them write the U.S. Mint—the agency in charge of producing U.S. coins. (Paper money is designed and produced by the U.S. Bureau of Engraving and Printing.) Have students pretend they are in charge of submitting designs for city or neighborhood coins. Have them write letters to the Mint recommending their locale and suggesting a design. Have them include reasons why their town or area is the best choice for a coin, and then create a two-sided design that illustrates and summarizes those good qualities.

Wayne Culp
1313 Mockingbird Lane
Arkham, North Carolina
27099

United States Mint
151 North Independence Mall East
Philadelphia, Pennsylvania 19106-1886

49

Coin and Purse patterns
(also use with bulletin board idea, page 16)

half-dollar front

half-dollar back

penny front

penny back

nickel front

nickel back

quarter front

quarter back

dime front

dime back

COPY and CUT

50

© Carson-Dellosa CD-2097

purse

SPECTACULAR SPRING BOOKS

Students are sure to know spring has sprung with these warm weather literature selections and activities!

Rabbit's Good News

by Ruth Lercher Bornstein: Houghton Mifflin, 1997. (Picture book, 32 pg.)

Rabbit hears something calling her and hops off to follow the soft, green sound. She discovers the voice of Spring through encounters with a worm, a flower, a baby bird, and others. Realizing that spring has arrived, she races home to tell everyone the exciting news.

The author and illustrator, Ruth Lercher Bornstein, used oil pastels to create the soft colors of spring and blended hues of the sunrise. Encourage students to notice the sunrise that progresses throughout the story, and the clouds shaped like little bunnies, then make their own spring pictures. Provide white paper and oil pastel crayons and instruct the children to draw a green horizon line across their papers. Then, have each child draw signs of spring, like the ones Rabbit saw, in the bottom half of her picture. Fill in around the spring items with green grass, using the side of the pastel crayon. Have each student draw bands of color across the top of the page to make a sunrise. After the pictures are complete, have students use tissues to rub across their pictures, blending the colors together. Display the stories beside each other around the classroom, matching up horizon lines, to make one large spring sunrise.

The Umbrella Day

by Nancy Evans Cooney: Putnam Pub., 1997. (Picture book, 32 pg.)

When Missy's mother predicts an umbrella day, Missy has to carry the big, old, dusty umbrella from the back of the closet. When it begins to rain, the umbrella, coupled with Missy's imagination, sends her on wild adventures in the circus and on the sea.

Let students' imaginations go on an adventure with an umbrella, just like Missy's. Draw a simple umbrella and copy it for each child. Have her color and cut it out and glue it to a piece of paper. Next, challenge her to draw a scene around the umbrella, using it in a way other than how it is traditionally used; for example, as a top for a carousel. Then, have each child write an adventure story about her picture, including how the umbrella became what it did, what happened, and how it became an umbrella again. Let students share their stories with the class, using a real umbrella as a prop.

51

Listen to the Rain

by Bill Martin Jr. and John Archambault: Henry Holt and Company, Inc., 1991. (Picture book, 32 pg.)

Stylized watercolor illustrations paired with lyrical text describe the melody of a rainstorm from start to end. Experience the stages of the storm from its soft and whispering beginnings, through the roaring and pounding, to its quietly dripping end.

After reading the story, organize a rainstorm orchestra in the classroom. Have each child choose an onomatopoeic word to represent a part of a rainstorm. For example, *pitter-patter, boom, crash, shhhhh, drip drop,* etc. Then, acting as conductor, start the rainstorm with the students who have quiet parts, such as *drip-drop,* or *pitter-patter.* Keep those students going while more, louder ones are added, such as *crash,* or *shhhhh.* When all the students are making their noises, start removing parts, starting with the loudest, until the rainstorm dies down to just a *drip-drop* again. Finally, enjoy the silence after the storm.

Egg Day

by Joyce Dunbar: Holiday House, 1999. (Picture book, 32 pg.)

Dora Duck asks her farm friends to each bring an egg to an Egg Day celebration, confounding the pig, goat, and horse as they try to produce eggs for the occasion. When Egg Day arrives, the animals go to surprise Dora with their eggs, courtesy of Hetty Hen, but Egg Day has already become Duckling Day!

Decorate eggs and celebrate Egg Day! Write an animal name for each student on a slip of paper and place in a bag. Give each student an egg pattern (page 29) on white paper, then let her pick an animal name from the bag. She must then decorate her egg to look like the egg of her animal, as if the animal laid eggs, just like the characters in the story. When all the eggs are decorated, display them together on a bulletin board and challenge the class to guess the name of the animal who "laid" each egg.

Mud

by Mary Lyn Ray: Harcourt Brace & Company, 1996. (Picture book, 32 pg.)

Spring melts the winter Earth and water flows over the land making wonderful mud. A child revels in this squishy soup as he squeezes it, stirs it, and dances in it. The earthy, textured illustrations match the tone of the book as the Earth is transformed from gloomy brown to bright green.

After reading the story, make some edible "mud" for students to squish. First, ask students to draw spring pictures and set aside. Then, mix 2-3 batches of instant chocolate pudding according to package directions. Have each child put on a smock, roll up his sleeves and dig in to a bowl of pudding. Let him squeeze it between his fingers and stir it with a wooden spoon, enjoying the "mud" like the child in the story. Record students' reactions, in writing or on a tape recorder, as they play in the pudding. Then, using the pudding mud as finger paint, let students paint some mud on their spring pictures. Set pictures aside to dry overnight and display around the room along with quotes from students during the experience.

Spring: A Haiku Story

compiled by George Shannon: William Morrow & Co., 1996. (Poetry book, 32 pg.)

Colorful folk-art paintings complement each poem in this collection celebrating spring. The poems are arranged to read like the story of a walk on a spring day. The poems are translated from traditional Japanese haikus, some more than three hundred years old.

After reading the book, have students create their own spring walk haiku story. Assign each child a part of the story. For example, parts could be: opening the door, walking outside, beginning the walk, during the walk, returning home, nearing the house, going inside. Assign several students to the middle of the walk. Next, ask each child to write a haiku poem reflecting his part of the story. Remind students that haiku is three lines with a 5-7-5 syllable pattern. After writing, have him illustrate his haiku. Compile the poems and pictures together in sequence to complete the haiku story. Finally, read the finished story to the class.

Puddles

by Jonathan London: Penguin Putnam Books for Young Readers, 1999. (Picture book, 32 pg.)

Two children go outside to play the morning after a thunderstorm. They explore the fresh, wet world left behind by the rain, playing in the mud, watching worms, following baby rivers, and best of all—puddle-jumping! They come home to dry off and get warm, only to head outside to splash some more.

You do not need rain to play this life-sized puddle-jumping game. Clear a space in the middle of the classroom and tape puddles cut from blue butcher paper in a trail around the area. Place numbers 1-4 in a bag, divide students into small teams, and ask each team to choose a member to be their puddle jumper. Line the puddle jumpers up at the beginning of the course, and then ask the first team a comprehension question about the story, such as, "What does Mama holler as the children go out the door?" If the team gets the answer right, they can pick a number from the bag and have their puddle jumper jump that many puddles. If the team does not answer correctly, another team may answer and pick from the bag. The first team to get its puddle jumper to the end of the puddle trail wins! Let the winning team take the book and read it to a younger class.

Spring Thaw
by Steven Schnur: Viking Penguin, 2000. (Picture book, 32 pg.)

Richly hued paintings depict spring as it makes its way across a farm, waking animals, melting snow and ice, and warming the Earth. The farmer and his grandson collect maple syrup and enjoy the warm glow of the sun on their faces. Spring has arrived at last.

In the story, the author describes the melting icicles along the edge of the roof as "a curtain of crystal beads." Turn a bulletin board into a farmhouse and have students make sparkly melting icicles to hang from the eaves. Form a house shape with colorful paper. Cut white paper in long, thick, bumpy strips and arrange at an angle at the top of the board to look like the top of a snow-covered house. A snow-topped chimney and windows can also be added. Cover the area above the house with a blue paper sky. Give each student a different length of white yarn, 12-18 inches long, and a handful of clear beads. Have him tie the beads at different spots along the yarn. Then, hang all of the beaded pieces of yarn along the eaves of the paper house, like melting icicles. Label the display *Spring Thaw*, and have students post their other spring crafts on the house under the dripping icicles.

SPRING THAW

54

Celebrate Earth Day

Teach students to love and take care of our planet as they celebrate Earth Day on April 22.

Did You Know?

- The first Earth Day was celebrated by the United States on April 22, 1970 to promote the preservation of the environment.
- Today, people in over 140 countries celebrate Earth Day.
- Rain forests cover only 2% of the Earth, but they contain half of all species in the world.
- About an acre of rain forest is destroyed every second.

Literature Selections

Dinosaurs to the Rescue: A Guide to Protecting Our Planet by Laurie Krasny Brown and Marc Brown: Little, Brown and Company, 1994. (Picture book, 32 pg.) Slobosaurus shows little respect for the environment, while the other dinosaurs show the reader ecological alternatives.

The Earth is Painted Green edited by Barbara Brenner: Scholastic Inc., 2000 (Poetry book, 81 pg.) An illustrated anthology of poetry that celebrates Earth's beauty.

Just a Dream by Chris Van Allsburg: Houghton Mifflin, Co., 1990. (Picture book, 48 pg.) After thoughtlessly littering, Walter has a dream about the future, where the world is an ugly and polluted place.

The Lorax by Dr. Seuss: Random House, 1971. (Story book, 61 pg.) The Lorax speaks for the trees, pleading with the Once-ler to stop cutting them down.

Recycle: A Handbook for Kids by Gail Gibbons: Little Brown & Co., 1996 (Information, 32 pg.) Clear, straightforward information about recycling.

A Piece of the Earth

Gaylord Nelson, founder of Earth Day, thought if people learned to appreciate and love the Earth they would work to protect it. Help students learn to value their home planet by finding wonder in a small piece of it. Ask each child to bring to class something special from the Earth, such as a seashell, leaf, etc. Have her observe it, draw it in detail, and label it. Then, under her drawing, have each child answer the following questions about her object: *What do you like about it?, How is it important to the environment?, What would the world be like without it?* If desired, ask students to return the objects to the Earth, where they found them, then display the pictures and writings on a bulletin board with an enlarged Earth pattern (page 63).

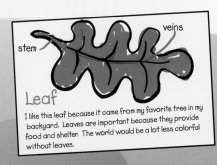

stem
veins

Leaf

I like this leaf because it came from my favorite tree in my backyard. Leaves are important because they provide food and shelter. The world would be a lot less colorful without leaves.

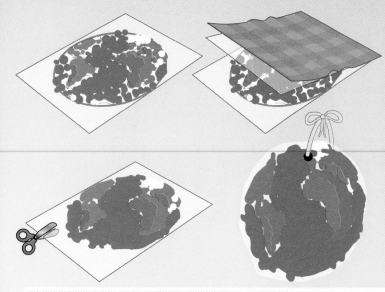

Earth Sun Catcher

Celebrate the beauty of our blue planet with eye-catching and sun-catching Earth ornaments. Give each child a copy of the Earth pattern (page 63). Instruct him to place waxed paper on top of the pattern and sparingly sprinkle blue, white, green and brown crayon shavings, using the Earth pattern underneath as a guide. Carefully place another piece of waxed paper on top, and a cloth on top of that. Have an adult press the layers with a warm iron, melting them together. Once cooled, let the child cut around the crayon in a circle, punch a hole at the top, and hang with yarn in a window.

Nature Journal

Make Earth-friendly journals to record observations and thoughts about the environment, like Henry David Thoreau did at Walden Pond. From 1845 to 1847, Thoreau, a writer, philosopher, and naturalist lived alone in a cabin near Walden Pond in Concord, Massachusetts. Every day he wrote in his journal what he observed in nature. His journal was the basis for his famous book, *Walden*, which helped peak people's appreciation for nature. Have each student choose a special place outside, either at school or at home, to observe daily and write about in a journal recycled from old worksheets and newspapers. Cut a sheet of newspaper 11" x 17" and gather several extra or used worksheets that have been printed on only one side. Arrange papers so the blank sides face up, then wrap the newspaper around them for a cover. Staple along the fold on the left side. Encourage students to share excerpts from their journals with classmates.

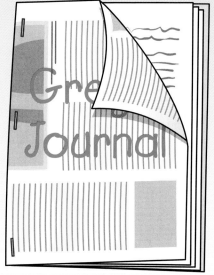

Endangered Species

In the past 200 years, more than 75 species of animals became extinct. Read the book, *Will We Miss Them?: Endangered Species* (by Alexandra Wright: Charlesbridge Publishing, Inc. 1991), then let students spread the word about endangered animals with these wraparound reports. Have students research and write a report about an endangered or threatened animal of their choice (refer to list below for suggestions). Next, have each student use construction paper to create a head, hands, feet, and tail for his animal. Tape the head above the report, the hands and feet to the sides, and the tail to the bottom. After sharing reports, let students display them on a bulletin board, grouped according to habitat (rain forest, desert, prairie, etc.).

Spider Monkey
Parma Wallaby
Giant Panda
Asian Elephant

Snow Leopard
Spanish Lynx
Northern White
Rhinoceros
Loggerhead Sea Turtle

There are two kinds of elephants: Asian and African. Asian elephants are endangered. African elephants are threatened.

Pollution

Pollution

The Earth is made of air, land, and water, and all three elements are polluted every day because of human actions. On the board, label three columns *air*, *land*, and *water*. Discuss the importance of each for life on Earth, and then brainstorm things humans do to pollute each area. Give each student an Earth pattern (page 63) and have her lightly color it with green and blue pencils. Cut a cloud shape from white paper and glue it behind the pattern to represent air. Then, using a black pencil, write pollutants on each area of the Earth, covering the Earth and cloud, to show how pollutants can destroy the beauty of our planet. Display the polluted planets with the title, *Don't Cover Our Planet with Pollution!*

Air Pollution Catcher

Even if the air around you doesn't look dirty, it may be! Let students test the air they breathe. Give each child a piece of poster board. Let her cut it into a shape of her choice, and punch a hole at the top. Next, cover the poster board cutout with petroleum jelly on the front and back. Thread a twist-tie through the hole and attach to a branch outside, so the card can blow in the wind, but will not blow away. Have students choose different locations around the school to hang their pollution detectors. Students may wish to make more cards and tie them to their parents' car bumpers. After several days, have students retrieve their cards and observe with a magnifying lens the particles collected in the petroleum jelly.

Water Contamination

Show students that even though water may not look polluted, it can still contain contaminants. Inform students that until the 1960s many farmers and chemical companies did not believe that unseen chemicals were polluting the water. Marine biologist Rachel Carson debunked this myth with her book *Silent Spring* (Houghton Mifflin, 1993). It revealed that DDT, a common pesticide, was seriously harming animals and the environment. Give each small group of students six clear plastic cups, a jug of clean water, and a dropper bottle of food coloring. Have students fill the first cup with water and add a drop of food coloring. Tell students that the food coloring represents a pollutant such as DDT. Next, have students pour half of the tinted water into the second cup and finish filling the second cup with clean water. Encourage students to record observations about the color of the water. Continue pouring half the tinted water into the next cup and filling it with clean water until the last cup is full. Students should observe that the final cup is almost completely clear. Ask students if there is food coloring in the last cup (even though it cannot be seen, there *is* still food coloring in the last cup). Relate the experiment to chemical pollutants in the water and inform students that water plants now filter drinking water.

Pollution Solutions

Earth-Friendly Cleaners

Keep your home environment sparkling clean without harming our environment. Harsh chemicals in commonly-used household cleaners can end up in the water, the ground, and even in our eyes and lungs. Copy the Earth-friendly cleaning recipes (page 64) for each child. Let her decorate the cards, cut them apart, and glue to used index cards for durability. Have students take the Earth-friendly cleaning recipes home to share with their families.

Composting

Teach students to reduce the amount of garbage put into landfills each year by composting. Explain that a landfill is a large hole that is filled with solid waste, such as paper, cans, food scraps, etc. Even though food and yard waste is biodegradable, often it cannot properly decompose in a landfill due to lack of moisture and air. Composting these biodegradable items reduces the amount of materials put in landfills and turns them into a rich soil that fertilizes plants.

To compost outdoors, alternate layers of soil, food scraps, leaves, and grass clippings and keep moist. Cover with a tarp in rainy weather. Mix the pile every week to aerate and circulate the materials to different areas of the pile.

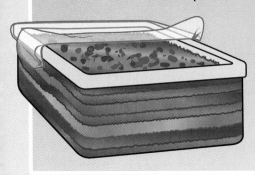

A mini-composting station can be made in a clear, plastic container. Add soil to the bottom of the container, and then layer yard clippings and food waste. Continue layering, sprinkling water between layers (do not soak). Cover with plastic wrap, pricked with a pin, and let the mixture sit for several weeks. Stir the compost each week and keep moist. Let students observe the materials decomposing in the compost. If possible, keep the mini-composting station in a covered place outdoors, because the decomposing materials may have a noticeable odor. Use the compost for class planting projects, such as *Sprout Necklace* (below).

Sprout Necklace

Clear the air by sprouting new plants in necklaces! Inform students that when plants make their food, they replace carbon dioxide in the air (produced by animal respiration and the burning of fossil fuels) with oxygen. Carbon dioxide in the atmosphere absorbs heat—keeping our planet warm for plants and animals to live. However, too much carbon dioxide in the atmosphere can make the Earth too hot—a condition some scientists refer to as *global warming*. Ask each child to bring in a small clear plastic bottle, such as a film canister. Wet a piece of cotton or paper towel and place inside the bottle along with two or three easy-to-grow seeds, such as radish or marigold. Replace the cap, tie a string around the bottle, and tie the ends together to form a large loop. Let students wear their sprout necklaces until they germinate, then plant the seeds in a flowerpot, using the compost from the *Composting* activity (above).

Lighten Your Load

The average American produces four pounds of trash every day. Work to reduce the amount of trash students produce at school. For one day, have students place as much of their garbage as possible in the same trash bag, including trash from lunch, paper towels from the bathroom, and any papers, pencils, etc., thrown away in class. To easily measure the weight of the trash, weigh a student volunteer first with and then without the trash bag. Have students subtract the second measurement from the first to determine the weight of the garbage. Record the weight of the garbage and the date. Then, encourage students to work on reducing their trash (see *Slash the Trash* below for ideas). At the end of the week, repeat the experiment and see how much garbage was reduced. If desired, weigh items that your class collects for recycling so students can see what they have saved from the landfill. Have students try the same experiments at home to encourage their families to reduce trash production.

Slash the Trash

Start a classroom campaign to *slash the trash*. Have students brainstorm ways they can reduce trash at school. For example: write on fronts and backs of paper, bring a lunch box instead of a paper bag, use pencils after the eraser is gone, etc. Write the trash reducing tips on the board as reminders. Do your part by having a week of no worksheets, giving students oral assignments, writing assignments on the board, etc. Test the class's efforts with *Lighten Your Load* (above). Have children visit other classrooms, telling students how they can slash the trash!

Redesign Packaging

More than one third of U.S. garbage comes from packaging. Challenge students to redesign the packaging of several products in ways that would reduce garbage. Give pairs of students a packaged product, such as cereal, potato chips, a boxed toy, etc. Have each pair look at the product and its packaging, and determine what parts of the packaging are not necessary. Ask students to design packages for their products that use less material or recyclable material. Have each pair present their new packaging to the class. Older students may wish to write letters to the companies that package the products, informing them of their ideas. Remind students that they can also reduce the use of packaging materials by not taking a bag when items can be carried out of a store without one or by bringing reusable bags when shopping.

Conserve & Preserve

Eco-School

Invite students to bring containers and old "junk" from home to turn into useful and fun school helpers. In addition to the following suggestions, challenge students to come up with their own ideas for using the materials.

Plastic Milk Jugs

- Cut jug diagonally at bottom to make a scoop. Two scoops can also be used as a toy to toss a ball back and forth. (Make a newspaper ball and wrap with tape to secure.)
- Poke holes in the jug, opposite the handle, to make a watering can for watering a class garden.
- Use caps as checkers on a homemade checkerboard.

Plastic Bottles

- Cut off tops and use as funnels in science experiments.
- Use caps as math manipulatives.
- Cut two bottles in half. Wedge together to make a terrarium.

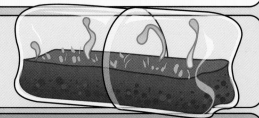

Boxes

- Cut cereal boxes diagonally to make class file folders.
- Cut and glue different shaped boxes (cereal, oatmeal, shoe, etc.) together to make a play castle.
- Glue boxes together to make a doll house. Make furniture from smaller boxes, spools, lids, etc. Glue on odd objects, such as toothpaste caps, beads, fabric, etc., for details.

Six-Pack Rings

- Make a ring toss by sticking old pencils into a box or piece of plastic foam. Cut apart rings and toss onto pencils.
- Use as stencils for drawing circles in art projects.
- Cut apart and make bracelets, gluing on sequins, glitter, etc.

Paper Bowls

The most common type of trash in landfills is newspaper. Students can unclutter landfills by reusing or recycling newspaper that is often used for just one day. Let each student cut old newspapers into 1" x 5" strips and grease the outside of a plastic bowl with petroleum jelly. Mix 1 part flour to 2 parts cold water in a shallow dish. Dredge a strip of newspaper into the mixture, and then press onto the greased bowl. Cover the bowl with two layers of strips. Let the bowl dry for a day, then add two more layers. Let dry completely, then slip the paper bowl off the plastic bowl. Paint the paper bowls with poster paint.

 # ♻ Recycle ♻

Celebrate Earth Day

What Will it Be?

What will a soda bottle become? To find out, have students collect plastic items with recycling symbols on them. Look at the number in the middle of the symbol to determine the kind of plastic from which the item was made. Each kind of plastic is sorted at the recycling center and can be used to make different things. Have students refer to the list below to find out what the future of some of the plastic items might be. For example, a soda bottle made from type #1 plastic can be made into any of the items beside #1. Ask each child to choose an item and tell a story about the life-cycle of the object, from what it is now, through the recycling process, to what it might become.

1 carpets, insulating material in coats and sleeping bags, bottles, containers, scouring pads, auto parts, paint brushes, industrial paints

2 detergent and engine oil bottles, trash cans, drainage pipes, plastic lumber, traffic cones, flower pots, combs, pails, recycling bins

3 drainage pipes, fencing, house siding, sewer pipes, garden hoses, traffic cones, handrails

4 trash bags, plastic wrap, shrink wrap

5 car battery cases, bird feeders, furniture, carpets, grocery cart handles, garbage cans, recycling containers, auto parts

6 packing peanuts, reusable cafeteria trays, videotape cassettes, insulation board, desk accessories

7 benches, picnic tables, sign posts

The Incredible Shrinking Necklace

Students can design their own jewelry and recycle plastic at the same time. Purchase an old toaster oven at a secondhand store (the project will make the oven unusable for food). Have students bring in pieces of number 6 plastic, such as plastic takeout containers or clear yogurt lids. Have students cut them into shapes, punch holes at the tops, and decorate with permanent markers. Have an adult heat the toaster oven to 325° and place the decorated plastic shape on aluminum foil, marker side up. Place the foil in the heated oven for about five minutes, or until the plastic has shrunk. Using an oven mitt, carefully remove the plastic and foil from the oven. Let cool completely, then have students tie string or ribbon through the holes and wear their recycled necklaces.

New From Old

Recycle old crayon stubs instead of buying new ones. Have students sort old crayons by color and peel off the paper. Place each color in a clean, dry, soup can (remove the label first). Use pliers to pinch a spout on one side. Have an adult place a saucepan with 2" of water on medium to low heat, and place a can of crayons in the water. When the wax has melted, have the adult use an oven mitt to carefully pour the wax into a paper-lined muffin pan. When the crayons are completely cool, pop them out of their molds and color! Remember to recycle the can and paper liners!

61

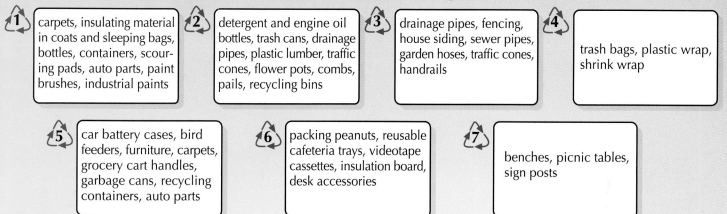

Conserve & Preserve

Conservation Cops

Resources on Earth are limited and many cannot be replaced. Teach students that saving water and energy is not only good for the Earth, but is easy, too! Read the book *Dinosaurs to the Rescue* by Laurie Krasny Brown (Little Brown & Co., 1994) and if desired, provide students with facts about wasting water and electricity. For instance, one flush of a toilet uses five gallons of water (show a gallon jug for reference) and 500,000 barrels of oil would be saved each day if every household lowered the heat 6°. Brainstorm things students and their families can do at home to help conserve water and electricity. Have each child create a poster with conservation tips and Earth-friendly designs, such as the Earth pattern or the recycling symbol pattern (page 63). Ask the children to take their posters home and encourage their families to follow some of the water and energy conservation ideas.

Energy Saving Snake

Energy is wasted when heat or cool air escapes through spaces under doors and windows. Show students how they can reuse old clothes to make cute draft stoppers and save energy. Gather enough pairs of old, clean stockings and tights for half the number of students in the class. Cut off the legs and give one to each student. Let her stuff the leg with the tops of the stockings and other old clothes or clean rags. Tightly tie the open end closed with a piece of yarn and decorate to look like a snake by sewing or gluing on fabric scraps, buttons, etc.

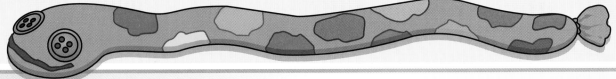

National Parks Project

Let students act as tour guides to teach classmates about U.S. national parks. President Theodore Roosevelt helped protect 230 million acres of public land as national parks, national monuments, wildlife refuges, and national forests. In 1916, the National Park Service was established to help protect the environment in these areas for future generations to enjoy. Divide the class into several small groups and assign each a national park to research, such as Redwood National Park, Everglades National Park, or Hawaii Volcanoes National Park. Have students learn where the park is located and what kinds of natural land formations, wildlife, etc., can be seen there. Then, ask each group to act as tour guides from their park and take the class on an imaginary trip to the park. Students may wish to make props of mountains, animals, plants, etc., to enhance their presentations.

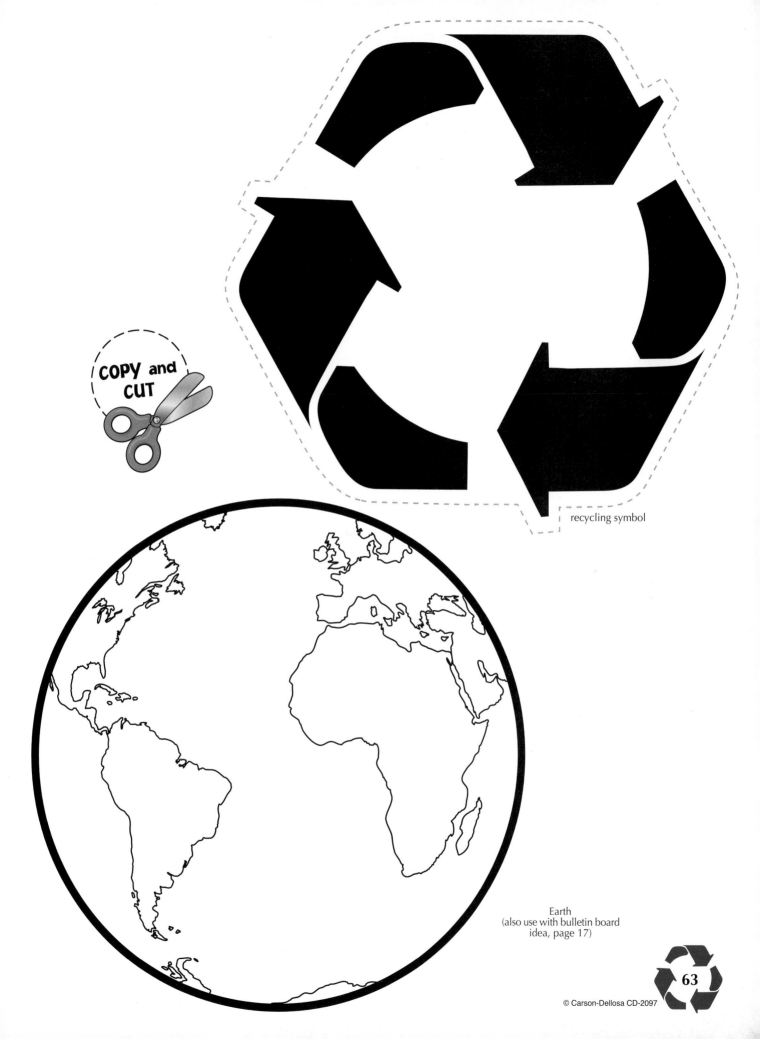

COPY and CUT

recycling symbol

Earth
(also use with bulletin board
idea, page 17)

63

Brass Polish

2 tablespoons flour
2 tablespoons salt
1 tablespoon water

Mix into a thick paste.
Rub with a soft cloth onto brass.
Rinse with water and dry with a clean, dry cloth.

Drain Cleaner

1/2 cup baking soda
1 cup white vinegar

Pour baking soda down drain and follow
with vinegar.
Cover drain until fizzing stops.
Flush drain with boiling water.

Silver Polish

Aluminum foil
Baking soda
Salt
Warm water

Place a sheet of aluminum foil in the bottom
of a glass bowl.
Sprinkle with baking soda and salt.
Fill the bowl with warm water and soak silver.
When clean, dry silver with a clean, dry cloth.

Window Cleaner

3 tablespoons white vinegar
4 cups water

Combine ingredients in a spray bottle.
Spray on glass or mirrors and wipe with a
clean, dry cloth.

All-Purpose Cleaner

4 tablespoons baking soda
4 cups warm water

Dissolve baking soda in warm water. Apply
with a sponge. Rinse with clear water.

Furniture Polish

2 cups olive oil
1 cup lemon juice

Mix together until well blended. Use a
clean, soft cloth to apply to furniture.

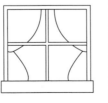

COPY and CUT

Earth-friendly cleaning recipes

ARBOR DAY
HAVE A TREE-RIFIC DAY!

Arbor Day is observed every year on the last Friday in April. It was founded by J. Sterling Morton, who wanted to see more trees in his new Nebraskan home.

Did You Know?

- If all morning newspapers in the country were recycled for one day, it would save 41,000 trees.
- Many countries have tree celebrations. India celebrates a "National Festival of Tree Planting," Korea has a "Tree Loving Week," Iceland celebrates "Student's Afforestation Day," and Israel has a tree-planting festival called "New Year's Day of the Trees."
- On the first Arbor Day, over one million trees were planted.

Literature Selections

Old Elm Speaks by Kristine O'Connell George: Houghton Mifflin Company, 1998. (Picture Book, 48 pg.) A delightful selection of poems that will not only introduce students to different forms of poetry, but also different ways to look at trees.

A Tree is Nice by Janice May Udry: HarperTrophy, 1987 (Picture Book, 32 pg.) Take a tour through endearing and sometimes funny reasons why trees are good to have around. A Caldecott Medal Winner.

Good Deed Trees

Plant seeds of community service with a tree planting ceremony at school. Pick a spot on school grounds to plant a tree. Collect money to buy a tree, and then take a field trip to a local nursery. Have students ask questions at the nursery to determine what type of tree would be best suited for the location chosen. Encourage students to consider factors like type of soil, amount of sunlight and rainfall, and climate. Send invitations to school staff and family members on recycled paper from *Safer Paper* (page 66). Divide students into two groups. The first group will help dig the hole for the tree. After it is planted, have the second group add soil to the tree's base. Have a student read a poem or dedication to the tree, possibly from *Old Elm Speaks* (see *Literature Selections*, above). If possible, place a plaque at the tree's base with the class name and date.

MRS. EDGERTON'S
FIRST GRADE CLASS
2001

Me Trees

Go out on a limb with these imaginative trees! Sketch a tree shape and provide a copy for each student. Provide baskets of assorted items that have naturally fallen from trees, such as bark, petals, pine needles, seeds, or leaves. Have students glue various items to the sketches and use crayons or markers to create their own trees. Then, have each student make up a name for the tree along with characteristics of the tree, such as what climate the tree likes or what type of fruit it bears.

Safer Paper

Introduce students to a revolutionary yet simple type of conservation: paper recycling. When paper is recycled, we use fewer trees. Make recycled paper with used scraps of paper (the more colorful the scraps, the more colorful the results). Remember that the scraps must be soiled only by ink because any other contaminates will disturb the process. Use the new paper in the *Trees Are Terrific!* books (page 67) or to make invitations to the *Arbor Day "Tree"ts* party (page 67).

1. Tear scrap paper into tiny pieces, and soak in water for 10 minutes.
2. Fill a blender with the pieces and cover with water. Pulse several times at high speed until the mixture is fine and thin. Mix with a spoon between pulses.
3. Pour the mixture into a large container such as a plugged sink or plastic tub. Add water to make the depth at least two inches. The pulp should be floating in the water.
4. Dip a piece of steel gauze or sturdy wire screen into the mixture, then lift it out of the water. Evenly distribute the pulp by holding the screen horizontally and shaking back and forth.
5. In one continuous motion, flip the screen onto a piece of felt so that the pulp adheres to the felt. Press the screen with a wet sponge to separate the pulp from the screen and lift it off, starting at one corner. Flatten the pulp with a wet sponge.
6. Allow the pulp to dry overnight and remove it from the felt.

Arbor Day "Tree"ts

Have an Arbor Day party to celebrate the anniversary of this day. Arrange a buffet of foods that come from trees, like almonds, pecans, walnuts, maple sugar candy, bananas, coconut, apples, oranges, and chocolate. Write the name of each food on an index card and tape it in front of the bowl. On the other side of the card, write the name of the tree from which it comes. Encourage students to guess the tree and then flip the card to see if they are correct. Send invitations to the party to family and staff members on recycled paper created in the *Safer Paper* activity (page 66).

oranges

almonds

cinnamon

apples

bananas

Good Reasons for Trees

Trees are Terrific!

Make a "tree"mendous book with your class! Brainstorm a list of why trees are valuable. If desired, use the *Literature Selections* (page 65) for ideas. Let each student choose one reason from the list to write about and illustrate on recycled paper. Have students read their paragraphs and share their illustrations with the class. Collect the completed pages and bind them in a book titled, *Good Reasons for Trees*. Display the book at the *Arbor Day "Tree"ts* party (above) for guests to enjoy.

Do Not Cut!

Trees Need Mothers Too

Give students something to "bark" about by letting them help Mother Nature. In this adopt-a-tree activity, students will appreciate all it takes for a young sapling to grow. Choose a tree already growing on school grounds. Label the tree *do not cut* to ensure the tree does not get cut down. Research the type of tree, let students draw pictures of it, and record what type of care it requires. Observe the tree seasonally and note the changes. You may consider having a school groundskeeper visit your classroom, and discuss the things he does to care for the tree. Have students alternate responsibilities in caring for the tree such as watering it, pruning it, pulling mulch away from its trunk, or adding mulch when needed. Create a log or chart in the classroom where students can record what they did for the tree each week.

It's Raining, It's Pouring!
Celebrate April Showers

Discover the science of weather and water with this series of rainy day adventures!

Did You Know?

- Water (H_2O) is made from two hydrogen molecules (H_2) and one oxygen molecule (O).
- We have all the water on Earth that we will ever have. No new water is made; it is just continuously recycled. The water molecules in your drinking glass could have evaporated from a puddle in China or a lake from which a dinosaur drank.
- Water is everywhere. Human bodies are 65% water and 75% of the Earth's surface is covered with water.

Literature Selections

Listen to the Rain by John Archambault and Bill Martin, Jr.: Henry Holt & Co., Inc., 1988. (Picture book, 31 pg.) Describes all of the sounds rain makes as it sprinkles and pours.

Rain by Manya Stojic: Crown Pub., 2000. (Picture book, 32 pg.) African animals use their five senses to predict when the rains will come.

A Rainy Day by Sandra Markle: Orchard Books, 1993. Informational book, 32 pg.) Using a picture book format, this book provides information on why rain falls, how clouds form, and much more.

Listen to the Rain

Plink, plink; splish, splash—it must be raining! The sound of rain can be described in many ways. Let students describe what they hear when the rain is falling. During a rain storm or a recording of a rain storm, turn off the lights. Ask students to close their eyes and focus on the sounds of the rain and how those sounds make them feel. Then, have each student write a poem describing his experience. Have each student share his poem with the class, then hang the poems on a bulletin board titled *The Sounds of Rain*.

> During a rainstorm, I am part of the audience, listening to nature playing large drums.

Puddle Pondering

The water cycle does not stop when the rain does. Let students examine the cycle firsthand. After a rain shower, take students outside to find a puddle on asphalt or concrete. Let a volunteer draw a chalk line around the puddle. (If no puddle is available, fill a few cups with water and place them on a windowsill. Draw a line to show the water level.) Have students predict what will happen to the puddle. Most students will answer, "It will dry up." Observe the puddle's water level over several days. What happens to the water? Does the puddle grow or shrink? Explain that the puddle shrinks because of *evaporation*—an important part of the water cycle. The sun evaporates the water by changing it into water vapor that floats in the air, and then gathers into clouds. Explain that without this process, there would be no rain.

Water in All Its Forms

It's a solid! It's a liquid! It's a gas! Water is the only substance found in all three states of matter at temperatures commonly seen on the Earth's surface. To examine the states of water, first have students cover their desks with newspaper and divide a sheet of paper into three sections titled *Solid*, *Liquid*, and *Gas*. Provide containers of water for groups to examine. Have students record their observations of the water, such as how it feels, its shape, where it is found, etc. Give an ice cube to each student and ask her to repeat the same observations at her desk. Finally, heat water in an open pan until steam begins to form, and have students repeat their observations. Ask students how water changes from solid to liquid (by melting at a temperature above 32° F), from liquid to solid (by freezing at a temperature below 32° F), and from liquid to gas (by boiling at a temperature above 212° F). After students make observations, challenge them to write definitions for each state of matter on their papers and give examples of other things that exist in each state of matter. Have students share their answers, then explain the scientific definitions: solids keep their shape and volume, liquids keep their volume but lose their shape, and gases have no definite shape or volume.

Cloud in a Bottle

Make it rain in a bottle! Assign students to small groups and give each group a large, clear jar with a lid, an empty aluminum pie pan, a flashlight, and ice cubes. Instruct groups to fill the pie pan with ice. Pour 1/2 cup of hot water into each jar, replace the lid, and place the pie pan on top of the lid. Let students shine their flashlights into their jars to represent the sun, and watch a cloud appear! As the clouds become more saturated with water vapor, they will darken in color, and eventually begin to "rain." Explain that the hot water warms the air, causing the water to evaporate. Water vapor forms at the top of the jar. The air becomes so saturated with moisture that it cools and *condenses* (turns back into a liquid), which causes it to *precipitate* (rain) inside the jar (water drips from the lid).

Just Add Water Molecules

Learning is "elementary" when students create water molecules. Explain that water is made from two *elements*—natural substances which cannot be divided into simpler substances. Explain that oxygen, a gas which animals need for breathing, cannot be separated into anything other than small components of oxygen. Water is not an element because it can be divided into oxygen and hydrogen. Give groups large sheets of blue and red paper, with a 2" circle traced on the red paper and a 3" circle traced on the blue paper. Have students cut out the circles and trace them to make as many red circles and blue circles as possible; then cut out the circles. Have students write an *H* on each red circle and an *O* on each blue circle. Tell students to tape the circles together to make water molecules, so that two hydrogen molecules slightly overlap each oxygen molecule. Finally, give each group an enlarged copy of the drinking glass pattern (page 74). Instruct groups to arrange their molecules on the pattern so that they do not overlap (provide extra glass patterns if necessary). Which group filled the most glasses?

Starring...the Water Cycle!

Go with the flow when teaching students the water cycle through dramatic play! Play this game in an open area, and use the water molecules from the *Just Add Water Molecules* activity (above). Assign the following groups, having them stand across the area in this order: clouds, rain, rivers, ocean. Give all the molecules to the clouds. Instruct "clouds" to crowd closer together, like water vapor making clouds. When they cannot get any closer, it has to rain! Have the rain take the water molecules and rush to the rivers, passing on the molecules. The rivers should rush to the ocean and hand off their molecules. Finally, the clouds should slowly walk to the ocean and retrieve the molecules, then start the cycle over again! You may wish to play a tape of a rain shower while the class completes this activity.

Raindrop Autobiography

What is it like to be a raindrop? Have students recap the journey in their own words! Tell each student to imagine she is a drop of water. Let her write and illustrate her life as a raindrop, using a separate sheet of paper for each stage. On each sheet, have her draw the raindrop's environment. If the raindrop starts out in the clouds, for example, the student would draw the sky. Next, give each student a raindrop pattern (page 74) to decorate. Let students illustrate covers for their raindrop journey books. Punch holes in the left side of the pages and loop blue yarn through the holes, starting at the bottom. Tie off the yarn at the bottom, and leave about 5" of yarn at the top. Attach the raindrop to the yarn. As students read the books, have them place the raindrops in each picture. Place the books in a rainy day reading center.

Where Does Rain Come From?

Everyone knows rain comes from clouds, but how does water stay in the clouds without falling? Clouds are made of tiny water droplets called *water vapor*. The droplets are so small that any air movement will keep them from falling. When the droplets collide and *coalesce*, or fuse together into larger droplets, they become heavy enough to fall as rain. Research types of clouds, then have students make cloud reference cards. The four categories of clouds are categorized by the altitudes at which they form: between 16,000 and 43,000 feet (high clouds), between 6,500 and 23,000 feet (middle clouds, which can overlap high clouds), at 6,500 feet and below (low clouds), and those with vertical development, such as cumulus or cumulonimbus. Give each student a piece of light blue paper to divide into fourths. Label each section with a type of cloud. Glue cotton balls, arranged like each cloud type, to each section. For example, students can pull cotton into wisps to represent cirrus clouds. Allow students to observe real clouds and predict the next day's weather. Let each child make several predictions, then record the results in a graph.

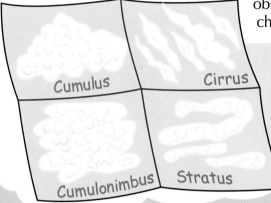

Cirrus (high): Light cirrus clouds mean weather will stay the same. Heavy cirrus clouds mean precipitation is coming.
Cumulus (vertical): Fair weather is ahead.
Cumulonimbus (vertical): Precipitation is certain if the cloud passes overhead. These are thunderheads; they are anvil-shaped and bring storms. Often form from cumulus (see above).
Stratus (low): Will bring drizzle or light snow.

Tomorrow's Forecast: Map it Out

The symbols on a weather map show what kinds of weather to expect around the country. Students can learn to read these symbols. Provide several laminated national maps and a copy of a newspaper's national weather forecast. Let students use construction paper to make the weather symbols for sun, clouds, rain, snow, and sleet. Post the maps and weather symbols on a bulletin board. Let children take turns reading each day's weather forecast, posting the symbols, and using markers to draw precipitation on the map. After your study of rain and the water cycle, compare the maps, and have students answer questions such as: *Did the rain move from one part of the country to another? Which parts of the country received the most rain or snow? Where will the sun shine tomorrow?*

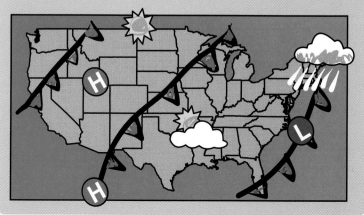

Catch Raindrops

Just like snowflakes, no two raindrops are exactly alike. Take students outside during a rain shower and allow them to "catch" a few raindrops on sheets of construction paper, then quickly go inside before the raindrops dry. Have students trace the shapes with markers, then combine the pages in a class book of *Caught Raindrops*.

71

What's Falling from the Sky?

Add interest to a typical rain gauge activity by measuring other rain phenomenon at the same time.

Rain Gauge Cut a clear, two-liter soda bottle in half. Turn the top half upside down and place it in the bottom half as a funnel. Attach a ruler to the side with a rubber band.

Clean Rain Gauge Place two lidless, clear jars near the rain gauge when rain is expected. Secure a coffee filter over the top of one jar with a rubber band. Check the jars when the rain subsides. How dirty is the rain in the open jar? How much dirt has been collected in the coffee filter? If there is dirt, what may have caused dirt to get into the rain?

Acid Rain Gauge Collect several clear jars. Have a student place a jar near the rain gauge at the beginning of a rain event. Periodically replace the jar in the rain with an empty jar. Check the rain in each jar for acidity using litmus paper. Tape the litmus paper to the jar, and label it with the time and date. (If litmus paper is not available, chop several red cabbage leaves and soak them in distilled water for an hour. Strain the water. Add 1/4 cup of cabbage water to every 1/2 cup of rainwater. If the rain is basic, the cabbage water will stay bluish-purple. If the rain is acidic, the water will turn red.) Test rain from the same rain event, keeping the jars in order according to when the rain was collected. Does the rain become more or less acidic as the rain shower continues?

Humidity Gauge

It's not the heat; it's the humidity! *Humidity*, the amount of water vapor in the air, is an important factor in determining the weather. High humidity means the air is saturated with water. Precipitation and condensation (in the form of fog or dew) are more likely to occur in humid weather. Choose a day that is neither too humid nor too dry to make a class humidity gauge, or *hygrometer*, and assign tasks to different students.

Materials: • small piece of lightweight cardboard
• 8" strand of human hair from a volunteer
• 9" x 12" sheet of corrugated cardboard
• 2 pushpins
• tape
• marker

First, cut a 6" pointer from the lightweight cardboard. Wash and dry the hair strand and tape it securely to the blunt end of the pointer. Use a pushpin to attach the pointer at its center point to the corrugated cardboard, about 3" from the top. Test the pointer to be sure it moves freely. Place a second pushpin about 5" below the point at which the hair is taped to the pointer. Wrap the hair around the pushpin, secure with a drop of glue if desired, and push the pin tightly into the cardboard to hold the hair taut. Use a marker to draw a 2" horizontal line, starting at the tip of the pointer. Write *low* above the line and *high* below it. When the humidity is low, the hair will tighten and the pointer will point upward. Because hair extends as it absorbs more moisture, in higher humidity, the hair will loosen, and the pointer will point down. Post the hygrometer in a protected area outside and let students check the humidity several times each day, and report the results to the class.

72

Rain, Rain, Don't Go Away!

Remind students that without rain, the Earth would be a dry, miserable place to live. Have a contest to see who can think of the most uses for the water that rain provides. Give groups of students blue, white, and gray construction paper, and have them trace and cut out several raindrop patterns (page 74). On the raindrops, have each group write a use for water, such as *drinking, generating power,* etc. Then, have students cut out puddle shapes and write ways to conserve water, such as *take short showers, repair dripping faucets,* etc. Have students paint a large outdoor scene on butcher paper. Post it on a bulletin board, and staple the student raindrops and puddles on the scene. Title the board *We Need the Rain!*

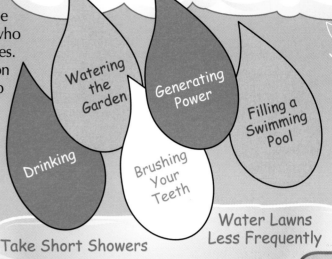

Watering the Garden

Generating Power

Filling a Swimming Pool

Drinking

Brushing Your Teeth

Take Short Showers

Water Lawns Less Frequently

Repair Dripping Faucets

Rainy Day Relay

Cure rainy day restlessness with an indoor relay! On a rainy day, provide several sets of child-sized rain gear (galoshes, raincoats, rain hats, etc.). Assign children to groups of four. In an open indoor area, hold relay races. Have pairs of students from each group stand at opposite ends of the room. The first runner on each team should put on the rain gear, run to her teammates at the opposite end of the room, then give the rain gear to the next runner. The race is over when the last runner on each team has dressed in the rain gear and run to the other side of the room.

Rainy Day Box

Rainy weekends can be as much fun as sunny ones, with a little preparation. Provide a large shoebox for each child to decorate using paint, construction paper, and reduced copies of the raindrop pattern (page 74). Let each child take his box home and fill it with things he likes to play with on a rainy day, such as a favorite book, art supplies, etc. Have students bring their boxes to class. Finally, let each child make a list of the box contents, as well as a short list of fun things to do indoors, such as make a tent from a sheet and furniture; play indoor hide-and-seek; learn a magic trick; write a poem about rain; etc. Post students' lists so they can write down each others' ideas to place in their rainy day boxes. Label the boxes RAINY DAY BOX and send them home. Let children report what they did after the next rainy weekend.

CRAYONS

RAINY DAY BOX

raindrop

drinking glass

COPY and CUT

raindrop

74

WILDLIFE

Sponsored by the National Wildlife Federation®, National Wildlife Week is observed annually during the third week in April. Let students explore the plants and animals that live in forest, desert, prairie, and wetland habitats.

Literature Selections

Where Once There Was a Wood by Denise Fleming: Henry Holt and Company, 1996. (Picture book, 32 pg.) Explains how wildlife is affected by building and development.

The Natural Habitat Garden by Ken Druse: Clarkson Potter, 1994. (Teacher reference, 248 pg.) Instructions and illustrations show how to create natural areas in grassland, wetland, dryland, or woodland areas.

Backyard Wildlife

Native plants and animals are part of the landscape in the desert, the prairie, the wetlands, and the forest. Let students observe the plants, climate, soil, and weather conditions in your area. Let them use this information to determine the habitat (woodland, dryland, wetland, or grassland) in which they live. Have students research the animals native to the habitat and make a class list of those they would like to attract to their backyards or neighborhoods. Explain that animals need food, water, shelter, and a place to raise their young in order to survive. Give students a checklist of animals and have them use their research to make a plan for attracting wildlife. Post the checklist on a bulletin board and have students keep track of the animals they see. Encourage students to take pictures and post the photographs on the display.

FORESTS

Forest Animals:
chipmunk, mouse, skunk, rabbit, squirrel, woodpecker, snake, salamander, deer, toad

DESERTS

Desert Animals:
tortoise, desert cottontail, elf owl, lizard, cactus mouse

WETLANDS

Wetlands Animals:
egret, spoonbill, pelican, crayfish, bullfrog, otter

PRAIRIES

Prairie Animals:
prairie dog, black-footed ferret, burrowing owl, badger, weasel

75

FORESTS

Did You Know?

Healthy forests contain both living and dead trees. Trees that have died but are still standing provide homes for birds and insects and other animals.

Forests located where the climate does not change drastically during the year can support more diverse wildlife, since most forest animals and plants cannot adapt to extreme temperature changes.

Forests are found in rainy, tropical climates (tropical rain forests); temperate climates (deciduous forests and temperate rain forests); dry climates (savannas); and wintry climates (boreal forests).

Literature Selections

A Log's Life
by Wendy Pfeffer: Simon & Schuster Books for Young Readers, 1997. (Picture book, 32 pg.) Painted paper illustrations show how fallen trees help regenerate forest soil and provide nutrients for new trees.

Counting on the Woods
by George Ella Lyon: DK Publishing, Inc., 1998. (Poetry, 32 pg.) Photographs accompany a poem about natural objects seen on a walk through the woods.

In the Woods: Who's Been Here?
by Lindsay Barrett George: William Morrow & Co., 1998. (Picture book, 40 pg.) During a walk through the woods, a boy and girl find signs of the wildlife that live there.

The Layers of a Forest

A forest would not be a forest without trees. Different types of trees and plants make up the five layers of a forest. Create a forest environment complete with trees, plants, and animals. Provide information and picture references about the forest layers (see right). Have students work in groups to draw and label the plants, trees, and animals in each layer on a large piece of butcher paper. Post the mural on a wall or bulletin board as children learn about forest wildlife.

Forest Layers:
canopy, understory, shrub, herb, forest floor

Animals:
hawks, crows, owls, squirrels, songbirds, tree frogs, bears, birds, deer, rabbits, mice, insects, snakes, earthworms, millipedes, slugs

Plants:
tall trees, young canopy trees, bushy plants with wooden stems, plants with soft stems (wildflowers, ferns, mushrooms, mosses, grasses), fallen leaves

Tree Houses

Trees are valuable members of the forest community. They provide food and shelter for animals such as raccoons, woodpeckers, squirrels, birds, bats, owls, and insects. Have students draw a large tree and post it on a wall. Provide materials for children to research the animals that live in trees. Let each student draw and cut out an animal and its nest, if appropriate, to post in the tree. Allow children to tell how and where their animals make their homes in the tree.

Grow Your Own Forest

Bring the forest into your classroom! Recreate a sample of forest soil in an aquarium or large glass jar. Place a layer of rocks at the bottom of the container. Add a layer of potting soil several inches deep. Transplant moss, small ferns, and other ground plants from the forest into the container. Keep the plants in indirect sunlight and carefully water them. If forest plants are not available, place craft store moss in the container and have students make paper ferns and plants. Place small twigs on the soil to resemble logs. Cover the container with plastic wrap, but leave a small opening on one side. Observe the miniature forest and talk about how these forest plants receive indirect sunlight because tall canopy trees keep them shaded. Explain how these trees also protect the delicate plants from heavy, soaking rain.

Logs provide food and shelter for forest animals like beetles, termites, and salamanders.

The Life of a Log

The forest has a unique and amazing way of producing rich soil for plants and trees. When old or diseased trees die and fall to the ground, they become logs on the forest floor. Have students make 3-dimensional logs that show the animals and plants that help recycle logs. Explain that animals, insects, and plants begin a process of recycling the log, returning nutrients and minerals to the soil so other trees and plants can grow. Give each student a copy of the log pattern (page 84) to color and cut out. Have him cut a long cardboard tube in half lengthwise. Glue the log pattern to the outside of the tube. Staple the tube to the bottom of a piece of heavy paper. On the outside of the log, have students illustrate plants that grow on the log, such as mushrooms, mosses, and fungi. Open the tube and illustrate the insects, such as beetles, ants, termites, and spiders, that live inside the log. Above the log, have students draw snails, salamanders, and porcupines, which make their homes near the log. When the logs are complete, have each student write on the paper how logs help plants and animals in the forest.

DESERTS

Did You Know?

- Deserts are dry places that get less than 10 inches of rain a year.
- Deserts can be made up of sand dunes or bare rocks and stones.
- Deserts are usually located in the middle of continents. Winds lose moisture as they move inland and drop very little rain over these areas.

Literature Selections

Cactus Poems by Frank Asch: Harcourt Brace & Company, 1998. (Poetry, 48 pg.) Poems about desert animals and plants are accompanied by striking photographs of desert wildlife.

A Desert Scrapbook by Virginia Wright-Frierson: Simon & Schuster Books for Young Readers, 1996 (Picture book, 40 pg.) An artist describes and sketches the plants and animals she sees in the Sonoran Desert.

Cactus Facts

Since water escapes from plants through leaves, cacti have spines instead.

Cacti are able to expand their stems to hold rain water. When filled with water, cacti look plump and full. After a dry period, they are much thinner.

Cacti usually bloom during the brief desert rainy season. The flowers are brightly colored or white.

Cacti come in many shapes and sizes.

A waxy coating on the outside of a cactus helps it retain as much water as possible.

Cactus Collage

When thinking of deserts, cacti often come to mind. Create a cactus collage by first having students cut oblong, circular, and tubular shapes from green paper. Share the *Cactus Facts* (at left) with students. Let each student glue the green paper shapes to a piece of brown paper to make his own cacti. Provide toothpicks for children to break and glue to the cactus to resemble spines. Let children cut flowers from colorful paper and attach them to the tops of their cactus plants. Combine all of the cactus plants to create a large wall decoration.

78

Call of the Wild

Coyote calls are a familiar desert sound. Coyotes are sometimes called *song dogs* because of how they communicate. Coyote calls are a series of whimpers, howls, barks, and yips. Divide students into pairs and have each come up with a call. Explain that coyote calls are used to find mates and offspring, to communicate with family, and to acknowledge other coyotes. One call can trigger responses from many surrounding coyotes. Have one set of students hide on the playground and howl. Let their partners use the calls to locate the hiding coyotes.

Desert Days and Nights

The desert is a place that comes alive at night. Most animals hunt for food at night. During the hottest part of the day, animals rest in cool places. Provide reference for students to find out the daytime resting places of nocturnal desert animals. Let students draw a daytime desert landscape, showing the animals in their hiding places. Instruct them to camouflage the animals so they will be hard to find. Let students trade pictures with a classmate and find the animals hiding in the pictures.

Desert Animals

Roadrunners, coyote, rattlesnakes, jackrabbits— these animals, among others, call the desert home. Have students create desert animal reference pages complete with illustrations and information about the homes of these animals, what they eat, and how they protect themselves. Provide reference materials and give students sheets of paper to draw and write about their animals as if they were really watching them in the desert. Instruct each child to use the reference materials to write a realistic journal entry about her animal's location and behavior. Cut a strip from a brown paper grocery bag and crumple it to make it look softer. Draw a diamondback rattlesnake design on the strip and staple it to the left side of a stack of journal entries, forming a binding. Title the book *Desert Adventures*.

Diamondback Rattlesnake

Home- burrow underground or under rocks

Food- eats small birds, rabbits, gophers, mice, and ground squirrels

Defense- makes a loud rattling noise to scare away attackers

Late one afternoon, I was walking through the desert when I saw something move. I quickly turned around and saw a rattlesnake coiled up next to a large rock. I stood very still and listened to the rattling sound of his tail. Suddenly, a roadrunner grabbed the snake and darted off.

PRAIRIES

Did You Know?

- Every continent except Antarctica has prairies, or grasslands.
- Elk, wolves, and grizzly bears were prairie animals at one time. As prairie land became more scarce, these animals moved to the surrounding mountains and forests.
- Fire is important to prairie plants. The seeds and roots of most prairie plants can survive fire and use the nutrients from burned plant parts to continue growing.

Literature Selection

If You're Not From the Prairie… by David Bouchard: Simon & Schuster, 1998. (Picture book, 32 pg.) Prairie life is described through poetry and complemented with illustrations depicting the different seasons and aspects of life in this region.

A Prairie Dog Town

Prairie dogs are familiar prairie residents. Members of the squirrel family, they are known as prairie dogs because early explorers noted they communicated using bark-like calls. Have students work in small groups to make a large prairie dog town like those the animals are famous for building. Explain that prairie dogs live in large neighborhoods made up of smaller families called *coteries* (COT•a•ries). They dig burrows deep in the ground and connect them to the surface using tunnels. A mound of soil is built above each entrance tunnel to be used as a lookout point. Have each group draw a prairie dog burrow and tunnels on a piece of butcher paper. Let students color and cut out a prairie dog pattern (page 84), write a prairie dog fact on it, and glue it to the paper. Then, combine all the homes on a classroom wall to create a large prairie dog town.

A Wide and Vast Prairie

Get a taste of life on the prairie! Many plants grow on the prairie, including shortgrasses, tallgrasses, and a variety of wildflowers, such as purple prairie clover, coneflowers, asters, and sunflowers. Have students recreate a prairie landscape in the classroom using pictures of prairies and prairie wildflowers as reference. Give each student an 11" x 17" piece of white paper and have him paint wildflowers. Instruct students to cut out the clumps of wildflowers. Create the tallgrass and shortgrass of the prairie by fringing large and small sheets of green paper. To make a prairie landscape, stagger the grass and wildflowers and attach them to a large wall or bulletin board.

Life Underground

With few trees, the only place for prairie animals to go is under—underground, that is. Have students illustrate these animals in their homes. Explain that many prairie animals, such as prairie dogs, snakes, ferrets, and owls, live in underground burrows. Underground homes keep the animals cool during hot weather and warm during cold weather. They provide shelter from strong prairie winds and fires and are a safe hiding place from enemies. **1.** Let each student draw a prairie scene on a large piece of paper. **2.** Cut circular flaps, leaving a small section attached to the paper. **3.** Have students draw signs above each flap describing a specific prairie animal, then draw tunnels connecting the signs to burrows. **4.** Have students attach another piece of paper under the prairie picture. **5.** Then, lift each flap and draw the prairie animal described on each sign. Let students trade pictures with classmates, allowing them to guess the animals using the clues, then lift the flaps to check their answers.

Prairie Poets

Inspire students to write about the beauty of prairie wildlife by showing them pictures of prairie wildflowers and animals. Have each student write a descriptive poem about the sights, sounds, and feelings the prairie evokes. Pair students and have them trade poems. Let each child illustrate his partner's poem. Call on each pair of students to show the two pictures and read the two poems aloud. Allow the class to decide which picture was drawn for which poem. Display the pictures and poems together on a bulletin board.

81

WETLANDS

Did You Know?

- Swamps, marshes, and bogs—better known as wetlands—are areas where the soil is covered with water or water is close to the surface at various times during the year.
- Migrating birds and animals stop in wetland areas for food and shelter on their journeys.
- Wetlands support as many different forms of wildlife as rain forests and coral reefs.
- Wetlands filter out impurities and pollution, keeping the water in rivers and lakes clean.

Literature Selections

Everglades
by Jean Craighead George: HarperTrophy, 1997. (Picture book, 32 pg.) A storyteller takes five children on a journey through the Everglades and tells of the area's past and uncertain future.

Squishy, Misty, Damp and Muddy
by Molly Cone: Sierra Club Books, 1996. (Picture book, 32 pg.) Large photographs show the plants and animals of the Everglades and the environmental importance of this unique area.

Sawgrass Poems
by Frank Asch: Harcourt Brace & Co., 1996. (Poetry, 52 pg.) Photographs and poems introduce life in the Everglades.

A Wetland View

Plants and trees that grow in wetland areas are partially underwater some of the time. Create an above and underwater view of life in a wetland. Tell students that decayed stems and leaves from plants become food for insects and fish, which in turn become food for larger animals, such as reptiles, birds, mammals, and amphibians. Begin by giving each student an 11" x 17" piece of paper. Have students draw a light pencil line across the lower portion of the paper. Provide picture references and let students draw the trees and plants that grow in a wetland, illustrating the bottom of the trunks below the pencil line (underwater) and top of the trunks and leaves above the pencil line (above water). Then, let children draw wetland animals, showing water and land animals in the appropriate places. Cut blue plastic wrap slightly larger than the bottom of the paper. Fold the bottom and side edges over and secure by taping them to the back of the paper. Post the wetland pictures on a classroom wall.

82

Save the Wetlands

Many wetland areas are in danger of being destroyed due to pollution and construction. The number of animals in these areas has sharply declined and several animals, such as alligators, wood storks, and panthers, are endangered. Encourage students to research and present public service announcements informing others about endangered wetland wildlife. Let each student choose a wetland animal and research how its habitat has been damaged. Have students dress as the animals and present their messages from the animals' points of view.

Design a Classroom Wetland

Introduce students to the wetland habitat by turning the classroom into a wetland wonderland. Explain that marshes and swamps are known as wetlands and are areas that are covered with shallow water. Create trees by rolling long sheets of brown paper into tubes. Secure them to the ceiling with tape and loops of yarn. Cut strips in the bottoms of the tubes, bend slightly, and tape each to the floor to resemble tree roots. Cut out *epiphytes* (E•pif•ites), or air plants, to attach to the tree trunks. To make sawgrass, fringe large pieces of paper and tape them to the walls.

Bird Watching

Birdwatchers frequent wetland areas to observe unique birds, such as egrets, ibis, wood storks, spoonbills, and snail kites. Provide reference books for students and have them draw and cut out life-sized pictures of wetland birds. Attach the birds to the display created in *Design a Classroom Wetland* (above). Go bird watching and have students bring special binoculars. Instruct each student to decorate two short cardboard tubes and tape them together using masking tape. Tour your classroom wetland and let children use their binoculars to spot birds, and then name the birds they see.

83

prairie dog

COPY and CUT

84

log

National Poetry Month

Robert Frost defined poetry as "serious play." Enjoy some serious play with your students during National Poetry Month!

Did You Know?

- Poetry is derived from the Greek word *poiein*—*to make*. The ancient Greeks used this word for any artist—writer, musician, painter—who created artwork that did not previously exist.
- Scholars believe that the literature of all cultures began with poetry. Poets were respected as keepers of traditions.
- In Britain, a Poet Laureate is named by the monarchy and writes verses for court and state occasions. In the United States, the Poet Laureate serves as a poetry consultant to the Library of Congress and is required to give one public poetry reading and lecture. The Poet Laureate is appointed by the Librarian of Congress.

Literature Selections

A House is a House for Me by Mary Ann Hoberman: Viking, 1982. (Poetry, 44 pg.) This rhyming picture book describes a variety of dwelling places for people, animals, etc., and provides an entertaining study of metaphor: "a rose is a house for a smell, a throat is a house for a hum."

And the Green Grass Grew All Around: Folk Poetry for Everyone by Alvin Schwartz: HarperCollins, 1999. (Poetry anthology, 208 pg.) A delightful collection of over 250 poems, limericks, jump-rope rhymes, riddles, and more.

Honey I Love by Eloise Greenfield: HarperFestival, 1995. (Poetry, 42 pg.) Short poems about the things and people that children love, including cousins, mothers, laughing, and water sprinklers.

The Random House Book of Poetry for Children selected by Jack Prelutsky: Random House, 2000. (Poetry anthology, 256 pg.) The 572 selected poems are short, but long on laughter, imagery, and rhyme. They are grouped around 14 categories that include food, nonsense, home, children, and seasons.

Class Favorites

"Gather flowers" to celebrate National Poetry Month! Inform students that the word anthology originally meant *flower gathering* (*anthos-flower*, *logia-collecting*), but now refers to a collection of literary pieces or works of art or music. As students read poetry, instruct them to choose 5-10 favorite poems to create a personal anthology, which can be themed, if desired. Instruct students to copy the poems and authors' names in their best handwriting. Provide résumé or other special paper for students to use. Students can illustrate the action of the poem or how the poem makes them feel. Have students insert the poems in a binder or folder and decorate the cover. Each child can write an introduction explaining why he chose each poem. Create a class anthology by having each child choose one poem from his anthology to add to a class book. Every day, read a poem from the class book or encourage children to recite or read to the class.

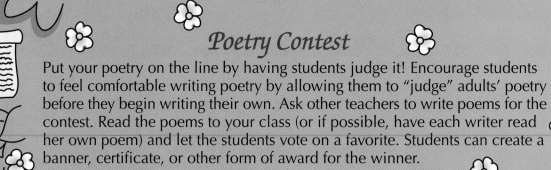

Poetry Contest

Put your poetry on the line by having students judge it! Encourage students to feel comfortable writing poetry by allowing them to "judge" adults' poetry before they begin writing their own. Ask other teachers to write poems for the contest. Read the poems to your class (or if possible, have each writer read her own poem) and let the students vote on a favorite. Students can create a banner, certificate, or other form of award for the winner.

All About Me

Let students begin poetry writing with a topic they know better than anyone else—themselves! Write the format for the poem on the board and have students write the poems on white paper. Let each student attach his final copy to an 11" x 17" piece of colorful construction paper. Take an instant photograph of each child to add to the work. Create a bulletin board display titled *We Are Poets and We Know It!*

First Name
Is (3 adjectives that describe you)
Loves (3 people or things)
Is good at (3 things)
Wonders (3 things)
Likes to eat (3 things)
Enjoys (3 things)
Laughs at (3 things)
Last Name

> Beth
> Is a fast runner, a quick thinker, a
>   roller skater
> Loves foot races, smiling faces, new places
> Is good at cartwheels, swan dives,
>   cannonballs
> Wonders about computers, compasses,
>   what's for dinner
> Likes to eat pizza, pizza, pizza
> Enjoys bike riding, puzzles, looking at
>   things upside-down
> Laughs at silly jokes, Mom's cartwheels,
>   Dad's dinners
> Layton

Class Poem

All together now . . . write poetry! Ease students into more poetry writing by making it a collective effort. Choose a topic that your class might be particularly interested in, such as kites, soccer, rainbows, etc. Ask each student to think of one line of poetry about that topic. Attach several sheets of paper together to form one long sheet. Give it to the first student and have him write his line, then fold the paper down and pass it to the next student. That student should write her line without seeing what the previous child wrote. When everyone has written a line, open the paper and read the collective poem to the class.

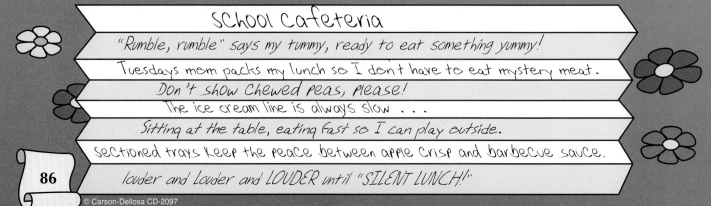

> School Cafeteria
> "Rumble, rumble" says my tummy, ready to eat something yummy!
> Tuesdays mom packs my lunch so I don't have to eat mystery meat.
> Don't show chewed peas, please!
> The ice cream line is always slow . . .
> Sitting at the table, eating fast so I can play outside.
> Sectioned trays keep the peace between apple crisp and barbecue sauce.
> Louder and Louder and LOUDER until "SILENT LUNCH!"

Periodical Poetry

Students can write poetry by choosing from words right in front of their eyes! Distribute magazines to groups of students and have them cut out 10-15 individual words. Remind children to include verbs, nouns, adjectives, adverbs, and articles, but do not tell them how the words will be used. Have students exchange words with a classmate and create poems with words they did not cut out. Give each child a sheet of poster board and let her glue the words to the paper to create a free verse poem. Free verse is a type of poem which conforms to no set rules; it has no fixed pattern of meter or rhyme. Display the completed poems on a bulletin board or wall.

Discover COLORS
Catch miracles
the secret place
on a young BUBBLE

Replace the Commonplace!

Jump-start students' writing by exposing them to new words! Develop a list of "tired," overused words such as *nice*, *fun*, etc. Let students use dictionaries and thesauruses to find exciting synonyms for each word. Have students write poems using at least five new words. Display the new-word poems on a "poet-tree."(Use the tree from *Easter Tree*, page 22.) Have students copy their poems on leaf-shaped, green construction paper. Bend paper clips into S-shapes and use to attach the completed poems to the branches.

"Do you want to know a secret?" whispered Tommy. "Yes," Billy yelled. "Shh! Promise not to tell anybody!" questioned Tommy. "Yes," Billy exclaimed. "I like Judy," Tommy declared. "You like Judy?" Billy shouted. "Oh, no." Tommy thought.

With glee my puppy runs liberated in the grass. His bark is cheerful and true. He follows an unfamiliar smell, a delicious red flower!

Fill-in-the-Blanks Poem

Star light, star bright. Ouch, a mosquito bite! Show students there's more than one way to complete a poem. Children can begin learning about rhyming patterns by working with parts of a poem. Give each student a copy of a poem whose rhyming pattern is AABB, such as Dr. Seuss's *Too Many Daves* or *The Wolf* by Georgia Roberts Durston. (*The Random House Book of Poetry for Children*, Random House, 1983.) Delete every even-numbered line and have students fill in the missing lines. Let students exchange poems to see how their writing diverged from the original piece and how their poems differed from their classmates'.

Original (blue) text quoted from the story *Too Many Daves* in the book *The Sneetches and Other Stories* by Dr. Seuss (Random Library, 1987).

Did I ever tell you that Mrs. McCave

well, she did. And that wasn't a smart thing to do.

come into the house, dave!' She doesn't get ONE.

This makes things quite difficult at the McCaves'

Did I ever tell you that Mrs. McCave
had a long beard and needed a shave.
Well, she did. And that wasn't a smart thing to do.
She cut herself shaving and cried "Boo hoo hoo
come into the house, Dave!' She doesn't get ONE.
hint from her husband how to make shaving fun.
This makes things quite difficult at the McCaves'
and probably will until they're in their graves.

Similes and Metaphors

Similes are as *easy as pie* and can be learned as *quick as a wink*! Inform students that a simile is a figure of speech that compares two unlike things. The comparison is often introduced by the words *like* or *as*. Ask students to think of fresh comparisons for *easy as pie* or *quick as a wink* or other well-worn similes such as *cool as a cucumber, warm as toast,* etc.

Like similes, metaphors compare two unlike things but do not include the words *like* and *as*. While the simile states that something is *similar* to another, the metaphor states that something *is* something else. For example, "love *is* a red rose." Call out words such as *book, picnic, recess,* etc., and ask students to think of metaphors for those words. Let the class judge the quality or power of the metaphors. Ask children how much additional information or feeling the metaphors give to each word.

When students understand similes and metaphors, let them choose a topic for a poem and follow the pattern below to complete the poem.

(Chosen topic) is (a color)	(metaphor)
It sounds like . . .	(simile)
It tastes as . . .	(simile)
It smells like . . .	(simile)
(Chosen topic) is . . .	(metaphor)

A cartwheel is green and
blue and green again.
It sounds like whoosh.
It tastes as fresh as
a honeysuckle.
It smells like grass.
A cartwheel is freedom.
        by Marty Rose

Onomatopoeia

Teach students to make word music! Introduce students to the sounds of language or *onomatopoeia*—words that sound like what they mean, such as *bang* and *zip*. Have students generate onomatopoeic lists for words such as rain, bells, wind, etc. Have them write poems using the word lists.

Rain
Plop in the puddle
I splash with my boots
Water drips from my hat

by Erin O'Shea

Haiku

Experience the balanced structure of the haiku! Haiku are unrhymed poems of three lines containing five, seven, and five syllables, respectively. They are usually light and delicate in feeling and explore nature or the season of the year. First, practice determining syllables by reading haiku and clapping out the syllables with students as you speak the words. Then, have students circle the syllables on copied haikus. Have students choose a topic, follow the pattern to create a haiku, and then illustrate it.

Haiku
by Amy Ravella

Mice are here and there.
Mice are almost everywhere.
This small mouse is lost.

Doodle Poem

Let students turn their doodles into works of visual and poetic art. Instruct each student to make a simple doodle on the bottom half of a paper. Then, ask them to think about what the doodle looks like and write a poem about it.

Doodle Poem

There once was a snail,
That was always so slow,
When the hare asked to race him,
He answered him no!

by Hayley Walker

Cinquain

Give me five! Students can write cinquain poems to honor their favorite spring activities. Cinquains are unrhymed, five-line poems that can be as varied as a poet's imagination. Instruct students to choose one-word topics and to follow the pattern below. Not all cinquains follow the pattern exactly, but all must have five lines.

Line 1 (2 syllables)—states the title
Line 2 (4 syllables)—describes the title
Line 3 (6 syllables)—expresses an action
Line 4 (8 syllables)—expresses a feeling
Line 5 (2 syllables)—another word for the title

Easter
Yellow, purple
Finding eggs everywhere
Celebrating a happy day
Joyous
by May Vellara

89

Nonsense Poems

A nonsense poem allows for some real serious play! Instruct students to choose two-word titles for their poems and compose several lines of poetry. Then, rewrite the poem by switching the beginning consonants of two words in each line. Let students read their poems aloud to the class. Have each child illustrate his poem on a separate paper.

> ### The Sellow Yun
>
> The sellow yun brings lays of right,
> And makes your day brappy and hight.
> The sellow yun brings hunshine to your seart.
>
> by Jason Gamble

Japanese Lantern

Write wonderful words with alliteration! Have students practice using alliteration when writing Japanese Lantern poems. Alliteration is the repetition of a stressed initial sound—usually a consonant. The Japanese Lantern poem should create a feeling and picture in the reader's mind. Have students choose a subject and follow the format, using words that begin with the same sound whenever possible.

Line 1 has one syllable
Line 2 has two syllables
Line 3 has three syllables
Line 4 has four syllables
Line 5 is the same as line one

Spring
Soccer
Saturdays
Special Season
Spring

Mobile Poetry

Create poetry in motion with these mobiles! Instruct each child to choose a title and follow the format below to create the poem. Give each child 10 colorful index cards and instruct him to write one word on each card. Draw a diagram on the board that illustrates how the cards should be attached. Have students follow the diagram, punching holes in the cards and tying them together with yarn.

Title–2 words
2 words
4 words
2 words

A
Vegetable
Green
Beans
Bad
from
a
can
yummy
fresh

Favorite Poem T-Shirts

Students can display their love of poetry by wearing poetry t-shirts! Have each child bring in a plain white t-shirt. Let each student choose a favorite poem and write the title or some favorite lines from the poem on the t-shirt, using fabric paint or markers. Allow students to decorate the shirts with sequins, buttons, or ribbon. Children can write *Natural-Born Poet* or *We Celebrated National Poetry Month,* along with the date, on the backs of the shirts and wear them during the *Poetry Reading* (page 92).

The Gingham Dog and the Calico Cat

90

Poetry Books

Create a keepsake poetry book for each child! Let students compile the poems they have written into books their families will treasure. **1.** Give each child a piece of tightly-woven muslin cloth approximately 13" x 19". Let students decorate it with crayons. **2.** Place two pieces of 12" x 9" cardboard on the back of the decorated cloth, fold the edges of the cloth over the cardboard, and glue with rubber cement. **3.** Place an 11" x 17" sheet of colorful, coated paper on a flat surface. Place several 11" x 17" sheets of colorful construction paper on top of the coated paper (use enough sheets for the poems that will be included). **4A.** Stitch down the middle of these sheets with a sewing machine to bind the pages together. **4B.** (If a sewing machine is not available, fold the sheets in half and use a push pin to punch holes about 1" apart along the fold. Use an embroidery needle and thread to whip-stitch the pages together.) **5.** Let students design a title page and table of contents for the book and draw a self-portrait for the last page. **6.** Glue the student poetry and illustrations on the remaining pages. **7.** Attach the pages to the cover by gluing the coated paper to the inside part of the cardboard cover. Include the poems from the activities on pages 86-90 in the students' poetry books.

A Gift of Poetry

Students will enjoy receiving a poem chosen just for them! Have students exchange names with classmates and choose a poem they think that person will like. Provide several anthologies or books of poetry. Teach older children how to use the indices if they are looking in an anthology for a poem on a particular topic. Instruct each student to copy the chosen poem on white paper in his best handwriting, roll it up, secure with a rubber band and tie with a ribbon. Let them present their gifts of poetry to their classmates. Alternatively, special poems could be chosen and presented to family members.

Classic Poetry

Children can understand and enjoy classic poetry! Choose a poem to share with the class, such as *The Tyger* by William Blake, *Ozymandias* by Percy Bysshe Shelley, (The Norton Anthology of English Literature, W.W. Norton and Company, Inc., 1986), *Stopping by Woods on a Snowy Evening* by Robert Frost, or *The Snake (A Narrow Fellow in the Grass)* by Emily Dickenson (The Norton Anthology of Modern Poetry, W. W. Norton and Company, Inc., 1988). Ask students to examine the poem for certain elements studied in class such as metaphor, simile, or alliteration. Ask students to explain why they did or did not like the poem. Students can write a response poem from another character's point of view, or tailor the assignment to the poem read. For example, if they have read *The Tyger*, ask them to write a poem that asks questions of an animal.

Poetry Reading

Poet Robert Pinsky once said, "Reading a poem silently instead of saying a poem is like the difference between staring at sheet music and actually humming or playing the music on an instrument." Hold a student poetry reading as a finale to National Poetry Month. Allow students to invite their parents and to advertise the event by creating and displaying posters around the school. Instruct each child to choose a favorite poem of her own or written by someone else and practice saying it aloud. Students could act out poems or dress up in costume to enhance the presentation. Prepare a program of student's names and titles that will be read. Dim the lights and serve refreshments for the special presentations. If possible, provide a spotlight and a microphone and videotape the readings.

Favorite Poem Project

Students might not know it, but many adults have a favorite poem! Ask each student to question a parent, another adult, or each other to find someone who has a favorite poem. If desired, provide a list of anthologies (see *Literature Selections*, page 85) for students to share with parents. Remind students that some songs are poems set to music and could be chosen as favorite poems. Have each student copy the person's favorite poem and ask the person to write a few lines about why it is their favorite. After reviewing the poems, let each student read his poem to the class and the reason it was chosen. Compile the poems into a class anthology for students to take home and share with their families. The activity will demonstrate that people around them are attached to poems and it will expose students to several poems they have not known.

Passover

Passover, a Jewish holiday celebrated for eight days, commemorates the Jewish peoples' deliverance from slavery in Egypt. Special foods are eaten at a *Seder* (SAY•der), a meal at which the story of the exodus is told. The foods eaten at the ceremonial part of the meal have special meanings. The matzo crackers—unleavened bread—represent the rushed escape from Egypt, which allowed no time for dough to rise. The egg symbolizes rebirth and new life. Horseradish, a bitter root, symbolizes the bitterness of slavery. *Charoset* (ha•RO•set), a mixture of apples, raisins, and nuts, represents the mortar used by the Hebrew slaves in Egypt. Parsley, a reminder that Passover occurs in spring, is dipped in salt water to represent the tears of slavery and the parting of the Red Sea. The bone and the wine represent the blood of the lamb which saved the Hebrew people.

Find the Afikomen

Give students a taste of Passover with this game. During the Seder, it is customary to have three matzo crackers in the center of the table. The middle matzo is broken in half. Half is placed with the other matzo and the other half is hidden and then searched for by the children. This half of the middle matzo cracker is called the *Afikomen* (ah•fee•KO•men). The child who finds the Afikomen is rewarded with a prize. Make matzo crackers by folding pieces of brown construction paper in half. Punch four rows of six holes each in the folded paper. Unfold the paper and weave yarn in and out of the holes; tie off both ends. Hide the crackers and let students search for them. After each student has found a matzo cracker, reward the class with *Matzo Ball Soup* (below).

Seder Plate

Let students make replicas of the ceremonial foods served at a Seder. Give each student a paper plate and have him cut out a bone and an egg from white construction paper. Crumple green tissue paper to represent parsley and white tissue paper to represent horseradish. Cut small squares from brown paper to symbolize the charoset. Let students glue the items to the plates.

Matzo Ball Soup

A special dinner is enjoyed after the ceremonial part of the Seder. The meal concludes with the traditional wish, "Next year in Jerusalem!" Serve this soup to acquaint students with a traditional Passover food.

In a small bowl, blend 2 eggs and 2 tablespoons oil. Add $\frac{1}{2}$ cup matzo meal and mix well. Refrigerate for 15 minutes. In a 4-quart pot, bring $2\frac{1}{2}$ quarts water and 2 teaspoons salt to a boil. Wet hands and form the batter into 12 balls approximately 1" in diameter. Drop into the boiling water; cover; reduce heat and simmer for 20 minutes. Remove the matzo balls from the cooking water with a slotted spoon. Add the matzo balls to 6 cups chicken broth and serve.

April Fool's Day

April Fools' Day originated in France, where it is celebrated as *Poisson d'Avril* (PWA•sawn DA•vreel) or *April Fish*. Until the mid-1500s, people in France (and most of Europe) celebrated New Year's Day between March 25 and April 1. King Charles IX and Pope Gregory XIII, among others, decided to "fix" the old Julian calendar by moving New Year's Day to January 1. Many people did not get news of the change or refused to follow the new Gregorian calendar, and continued to celebrate New Year's on April 1. Considered foolish by their friends, they were given invitations to fake New Year's parties, sent on "fool's errands" to find impossible things, and were victims of numerous practical jokes. The tradition of tricking people on April 1 rapidly spread throughout Europe and then to America.

My Dog Ate It?

Start off your study of April Fool's Day with a practical joke of your own! With a straight face, give your students a ridiculous or impossible assignment to complete, or ask them to turn in a project that you never assigned. Wait for their (presumably outrageous) reactions, then explain to them the real assignment— a narrative writing contest to see who can come up with the most creative excuse for not having their "homework." Have students share their work with the class.

Foolish Phrases

April Fool's Day is a great time to take pleasure in wordplay, jokes, and puns. Give students a chance to turn words of wisdom wacky. Brainstorm proverbs, clichés, and popular sayings and write them on the board. Have students discuss the meanings and possible origins of these phrases. Next, ask students to choose 5-10 sayings to rewrite with new endings, such as *A penny saved... is not as good as a dollar saved, A bird in the hand… sounds risky*, and *I think, therefore… I have a headache*. Let students read their favorite foolish phrases aloud for laughs.

Foolish News

One famous practical joke was played on the public by the British Broadcasting Company in 1957 when a reliable news program aired a documentary about harvesting spaghetti trees and showed workers "picking" pasta from real trees! Have students think up hilarious headlines and fictitious news stories of their own. Collect strange and unusual true stories and compile them with students' original stories. Read the articles aloud and have students guess which stories are true.

PASTA TREE HARVEST

Fool's Errands

In France, people who were tricked into attending nonexistent New Year's parties in April were said to be on *fool's errands*. The custom quickly became a contest to see who could trick another person into attempting the most impossible or useless (but believable) task. Let students write imaginative problem solving stories about doing the impossible—succeeding at a fool's errand. Brainstorm a list of impossible tasks and list them on the board. Let each student select one task as the premise for a narrative adventure. Potential errands might include catching rain in a sieve, finding a needle in a haystack, counting the grains of sand on a beach, or moving a mountain. Encourage students to imagine that anything is possible!

Pin the Fish Game

A popular tradition in France on April 1 is for children to hang a paper fish on an adult's back without getting caught. If successful, the child yells, "Poisson d'Avril!" or "April Fish!" and is rewarded with a piece of candy. Play a *Pin the Fish* game similar to *Pin the Tail on the Donkey*. First, draw a life-sized human shape on bulletin board paper. Give each student a piece of construction paper and let her draw and cut out a colorful fish. Attach a piece of clear tape to each fish. Have students take turns being blindfolded and spun around, and let them try to place the fish on the target. If they succeed, have everyone shout "Poisson d'Avril!" Reward each successful student with a piece of candy or other prize.

The Feast of Valborg

The Feast of Valborg takes place in Sweden on April 30. The Feast of Valborg is not really a feast, but a celebration of the coming of spring and light. This holiday is celebrated primarily by university students, who gather at Sweden's oldest university to make speeches and sing songs praising spring. Students put on white hats to symbolize the changing of winter to spring. In some places, students make floats commemorating events of the past year. People light bonfires on this night, dance, and listen to choral singers.

Hats on to Spring!

Welcome spring with these headbands! The traditional Feast of Valborg hat looks like a sailor's hat with a flower decoration on the band.

To make headbands, give each student a 2" wide strip of white paper long enough to fit around her head with approximately 1" left at each end. Provide construction paper, sequins, markers, etc., for students to decorate the strips. Students may wish to draw symbols of spring, such as flowers, birds, trees, etc., on their strips. After students have finished decorating the strips, glue or tape the ends together to form a headband. Let students don their hats and say "Welcome!" to spring.

Sing to Spring!

Many people sing songs to spring during the Feast of Valborg. Let students sing the following song to honor this tradition. If desired, have students make up their own songs for spring.

Hello, Spring!
(sing to the tune of *Twinkle, Twinkle Little Star*)
Spring has finally come to town,
Blooming flowers all around.
Birds are singing in the trees,
Buzzing, buzzing are the bees.
Spring has finally come to town,
Blooming flowers all around.

Spring Welcomes

What's your favorite thing about spring? Find out what students think with this activity. During the Feast of Valborg it is customary to greet spring with speeches. Give each student a piece of paper and have him create a greeting for spring. Greetings may take the form of illustrations, poems, paragraphs, etc. Let each student share his greeting with the class and explain the meaning behind it. Post the greetings on a bulletin board titled *Our Favorite Things About Spring!*